Recovery

Exercises

For Christians

Book Two

Ken Gross

This page intentionally left blank.

Recovery Exercises for Christians

Book Two

50 Written Exercises

Based on Scriptural Principles

From the Books of Wisdom

Psalms, Proverbs and Ecclesiastes

Thank you Kathy Trout, my friend, co-worker in helping

others and editor of this book.

Notice – This book of written exercises is designed to be used by those in some form of recovery program and under the guidance of a sponsor, mentor, coach or counselor. It is written with the understanding that the publisher and author are not engaged in rendering any form of professional services. The exercises provided in this book are meant to be used by an individual or a group for study purposes, and they are not in any way designed to be a substitute for one-to-one professional therapy if such help is necessary.

About the Author

Ken was born in the UK, and at age three developed tuberculosis resulting in him being taken by his family to a sanitarium for treatment. This action of abandonment, although it saved his life, set him on a path that contained many struggles, and eventually led to recovery in his own life.

Before he got there, recovery, he obtained an undergraduate degree with a joint major in Chemistry and Physics from the University of London and an MBA from the University of Oklahoma. He spent some time working in the water industry in the UK, then the oil industry in Saudi Arabia and finally in the financial services industry here in the US.

In 2009 God gave him the vision for a new style of recovery ministry and he became the founding director of Merimnao (merimnao.org) which he still runs to this day. He also wrote and published three recovery oriented books, the "Emotional Prison" series. The three book series covers how emotions trap us; looks at the major emotional prisons that exist, such as religion, false intimacy and perfectionism; and how to become free of the prisons, or healed. These books are available through Merimnao or on amazon.com, including a kindle version.

Ken is available at director@merimnao.org for those that may wish to speak with him, request him to train group leaders in Christian recovery leadership or request him to speak at retreats.

Table of Contents

Recommendations

For Sponsors, Mentors, Coaches, Pastors or Counselors

We recommend that those who are guiding others through recovery programs, a disciplined plan of spiritual formation, Christian lifestyle coaching or personal therapy use these exercises as an adjunct part of their work.

Every exercise is designed for the individual doing the work to provide written responses. They can be thought of as focused journaling, the writing down of specific thoughts and/or meditations relating to their personal plan of recovery or therapy in the context of God's word.

For 12 step program sponsors, although these exercises have a suggested step that the author believes might be appropriate, the sponsor can choose to use them as he or she sees fit. As such they help the sponsor to encourage their program participant look at a wide range of recovery topics more closely. We therefore suggest that the sponsee owns a personal copy of this book and the sponsor assigns exercises as appropriate, giving the sponsee time to complete one and coming back together to discuss the results and see what God may be revealing.

For Program or Plan Participants

These exercises are designed to assist and guide a personal introspection into an individual's heart, mind and will. This is always best done under the guidance of the Holy Spirit. This is why we suggest that before a person begins an exercise, they say a short prayer asking God through His Spirit to reveal what needs to be known or looked at in going through the work involved.

There is no right or wrong about any of the answers. The best results for a person doing this exercise come when they are open and honest with God, themselves and their program guide and give themselves time to do the work. Our experience suggests a minimum of a week per exercise.

General Instructions to Book Users

This is a workbook of sorts. While we have put in space for users to write in the book, the intent is for those doing the exercises to write their responses in other locations. Examples of this might be personal journals or recovery folders; something personal and private to an individual.

We do suggest that those assigning exercises might write in the book of a program participant or other end user. Sometimes encouraging words can be added; or extra commentary on the scriptures being used or possibly more individualized direction and instructions. Each exercise has space allocated for this purpose.

Being thorough in doing the work, as in all work, yields the most optimal results for an individual using these exercises. Use the book with a view to being healed from something or overcoming a serious struggle. This is the kind of thing that the Apostle Paul was talking about in Philippians 2:12-13. As we adopt this attitude of working with an expectation of the Spirit doing something in us, the work becomes a part of our personal sanctification; God's saving work that He performs with us and in us throughout our lives.

You may notice that some of the exercises may be similar to one another; this is by design. Our experience in recovery work suggests that looking at the same problem from different perspectives is advantageous in achieving good program results. Included in each exercise is a short list of emotion and attitude words that could be used in an individual's written exercise response. At the back of the book, Addendum 3 contains a good selection of emotion/attitude words for reference.

Finally, we suggest that an individual keep all notes, answers and responses separate and private from other personal documentation as these exercises will reveal things to you that others may not understand and therefore misinterpret.

This page intentionally left blank.

Exercise 1

Psalm 103:3-5

<u>Who Heals, Restores and Renews?</u>

Ps 103:3-5 - Who forgives all your iniquity, who heals all your diseases, who redeems your life from the pit, who crowns you with steadfast love and mercy, who satisfies you with good so that your youth is renewed like the eagle's. ESV

<u>Guiding Commentary</u> – This is a part of a Psalm that describes to us the answer to the question above. Obviously, the answer is God. If this is true then why do so many people act like they don't believe this? God is telling us right here that it is He who renews us; who gets us out of the pits we dig and fall into and who brings compassion to work in our lives. Only He can do this for us, only He can bring us full and complete forgiveness, only He can heal us in every way we need to be healed. Read the whole of this Psalm and let it speak into your life, it is the word of God about Himself, and shares what He will do and how He will do it in your life.

<u>The Exercise</u> – Have you been guilty of not believing that God can heal you, that He will forgive you and that He will restore and renew you? Write about the unbelief on these issues in your life. Start with the unbelief you had before recovery, then talk about how you came to believe some things about Him and His healing. Then write about some of the things you are struggling with now in the sense of unbelief that God will restore, renew and heal you.

Finally write out a prayer of request that Jesus will help you with your unbelief. Be sure to include a request for Him to show you where you have hidden unbelief or false beliefs in your heart. Be specific in what you are asking for, and be ready to share this prayer with your sponsor or mentor.

Sponsor Notes: _____

_____

_____

Useful Feeling Words:

- Renewed, Happy, Blessed, Redeemed, Free

Useful Attitudinal Words:

- Forgiveness, Hopefulness, Gratefulness, Joyful, Cleanness

My Pre-exercise Notes: _____

_____

_____

_____

_____

The suggested step for Exercise 1 is Step 4.

Exercise 2

Psalms 1:1-3

A Perspective on Recovery

Ps 1:1-3 - Blessed is the man who walks not in the counsel of the wicked, nor stands in the way of sinners, nor sits in the seat of scoffers; but his delight is in the law of the Lord, and on his law he meditates day and night. He is like a tree planted by streams of water that yields its fruit in its season, and its leaf does not wither. In all that he does, he prospers. ESV

<u>Guiding Commentary</u> –This Psalm provides a contrast between the righteous and the wicked. Here we are going to focus on the righteous aspect of Christ-centered recovery. This Psalm tells us that in recovery we will be blessed, meaning have success, based on five simple conditions. First, we are to avoid bad counsel which includes non-Christian therapists or Christian counselors who don't counsel from a biblical worldview. Secondly, we are to quit "acting out" and associating with those who lived in our former sins with us. Thirdly, we are to dissociate with people who don't believe in what we are doing, which is taking our problems to Christ and His people. Next we are to take joy in and have appreciation for God's word. The fifth thing we are to do is to study, pray and meditate on God's word and how it applies to our recovery.

If we do these things, which are a description of our part in our own recovery, there will be some results. We will become fed and watered, spiritually speaking, and we will yield fruit (check Gal 5:22-23 for a description of fruit) when God moves us into a new season in our lives. We will prosper, again, spiritually speaking, which means our souls will be functioning much better than they did before recovery. This will be most noticeable in the quality of our decision making.

<u>The Exercise</u> – Write about how well you have done in your recovery in the five conditions listed above. Separate each one out and for each condition write at least one paragraph, giving examples of how you have met and are meeting these conditions, naming names where appropriate and discussing any regular activities that you engage in to purposefully work on some of these.

When that is finished, write about the results of your recovery activities in the context of being spiritually fed and watered, spiritually prospering, your personal level of dysfunctions compared to the past and your decision making.

Sponsor Notes: _____

_____

_____

Useful Feeling Words:

- Introspective, Refreshed, Alive, Joyful, Blessed

Useful Attitudinal Words:

- Perseverance, Diligence, Expecting, Desirous, Peacefulness

My Pre-exercise Notes: _____

_____

_____

_____

The suggested step for Exercise 2 is Step 11.

Exercise 3

Proverbs 1:7

<u>Christian Recovery Begins Here</u>

Prov 1:7 - The fear of the Lord is the beginning of knowledge; fools despise wisdom and instruction. ESV

<u>Guiding Commentary</u> – This is really quite easy to understand from a recovery perspective. When we were "acting out" we didn't care about much other than ourselves and getting our "fix" of something. We certainly were fools, and we did not like people who tried to stop us from enjoying ourselves, and sometimes we even despised them. We had no fear of the Lord, and our attitude toward God was one of contempt. Then something changed as we began to experience the consequences of our actions. We entered into Christian recovery with at least a limited knowledge that God has ways of working things out for people who come to Him, and that He can heal us. We wanted to know things; we were tired of being fools. We wanted to know what to do to get healed. Some of us worked and worked and seemed to get nowhere, that is until we began to understand that we must develop a reverential attitude toward God, we must choose His ways over ours. For 12-steppers this is really what steps one, two and three are all about.

<u>The Exercise</u> – Discuss, by writing down, your level of contempt for God prior to recovery. Did you knowingly violate His commands and instructions? Was your level of contempt driven by attitudes of pride, rebellion, resentment, bitterness or maybe even disobedience? As far as you can remember, talk about all of those things and describe the kinds of thoughts, feelings and impulses that you had during your "contemptuous phase".

Now talk about where you are in your level of contempt for God. Do you still have some? Are you still carrying around some of those old attitudes?

Finally, write out your best description of your level of fear of the Lord. Describe what that term means to you. Do you believe God is dangerous for you, that He will cause you harm, or cause or allow bad things to happen to you if you don't knuckle under in your recovery?

(In exercise 4 we look at how to develop "fear of the Lord")

Sponsor Notes: _____

_____

_____

Useful Feeling Words:

- Anxious, Fear, Stressed, Tired, Alone

Useful Attitudinal Words:

- Passive, Weakness, Anxiety, Loneliness, Bored

My Pre-exercise Notes: _____

_____

_____

_____

_____

The suggested step for Exercise 3 is Step 3.

Exercise 4

Proverbs 2:1-5

Developing Fear of the Lord

Prov 2:1-5 - My son, if you receive my words and treasure up my commandments with you, making your ear attentive to wisdom and inclining your heart to understanding; yes, if you call out for insight and raise your voice for understanding, if you seek it like silver and search for it as for hidden treasures, then you will understand the fear of the Lord and find the knowledge of God. ESV

Guiding Commentary – In Scripture the "fear of the Lord" is linked to healing and living under the power of God, which is what all of us in recovery want (Lk 5:17). In these verses God tells us how to discern the healthy fear of the Lord He desires to see in us. It is a simple recipe; let's identify the parts of it. Receive His words (listen to Him, study the Bible); treasure His commandments (value God's instructions, note Ps 119:11); listen to wisdom (pay attention to Him and His word); incline your heart to understanding (check your attitudes to Him and His word); cry for discernment (pray fervently and like a child for knowledge and understanding of what God's word is saying to you); lift your voice (ask God and others to help you know Him and His word); and seek and search (God's word is precious and needs to be sought after because it contains hidden treasures). If each of us will do these seven things diligently, then we will have the fear of the Lord in us. That will put us in a great place for healing.

The Exercise – In this exercise we want to make an honest self-assessment of our "fear of the Lord", this is something we can then discuss with our counselor, mentor or sponsor in detail. Take each one of these seven activities and write at least one paragraph describing how well you are doing with it. Take time over this, be honest, seek God in prayer, and ask people who know you what they think about your level of commitment in these areas.

If you apply rigorous honesty to this exercise it will help you to understand where you are, spiritually speaking, and the Holy Spirit will point out where you can work in more proficient ways to receive the healing you want. In Christian recovery we sometimes forget that it is only God who can heal (help us become free from our bondages), having "fear of the Lord" puts our hearts in the place where He can show His healing power.

Sponsor Notes: _____

_____

_____

Useful Feeling Words:

- Overwhelmed, Fearful, Anxious, Ignorant, Apprehensive

Useful Attitudinal Words:

- Apprehension, Anxiety, Contentious, Angry, Ashamed

My Pre-exercise Notes: _____

_____

_____

_____

_____

The suggested step for Exercise 4 is Step 3.

Exercise 5

Ecclesiastes 1:12-14

How are you Striving?

Eccl 1:12-14 - I the Preacher have been king over Israel in Jerusalem. And I applied my heart to seek and to search out by wisdom all that is done under heaven. It is an unhappy business that God has given to the children of man to be busy with. I have seen everything that is done under the sun, and behold, all is vanity and a striving after wind. ESV

Guiding Commentary – This was written by Solomon, often called the wisest man that ever lived, which cannot be true, because Jesus was actually a man who had the wisdom of God in Him. Solomon nevertheless was incredibly wise. In this scripture he makes a global statement that everything man does under his own power is done in vain and we chase these things as if we were chasing the wind, which of course cannot ever be caught. This is a lesson for us in recovery. All of us have been chasing something "under our own power", or in our own strength. Most commonly, it might have been self medication through acting out with drugs, sex, gambling or something as simple as work in trying to achieve an emotional state where we feel better about life. Even in recovery, we are often chasing relief from our emotional pain and also healing, working hard under our own power to make "it" happen. Solomon lays it out for us here. He states that it is all vanity, meaning that it will not satisfy us and will actually leave us empty, and that we are wasting our time as we are chasing something that cannot be caught. Later in the book of Ecclesiastes he does tell us what will satisfy, God and God alone. The message here for us in recovery is that if we want to get relief, and become healed, we must strive in God's power, doing recovery His way, and then we will be filled, satisfied, and we will catch the prize of His healing.

The Exercise – Write out your own story of powerlessness in the context of this scripture. Write about your experiences in striving after your own relief from pain and the burden of your compulsions or addictions. Are you bringing those old concepts of "I can do this by myself" or "I am powerful enough to handle my healing", into your work as if you can control the whole recovery process yourself? Are you really submitting yourself to God's methods and timing, or are you doing recovery your own way? Maybe you used to "do recovery" under your own power and discovered that you were really powerless. Talk about when you realized that you couldn't go it alone, and that you needed others to be on the journey with you because God's power is manifested through other believers who are also in recovery.

Sponsor Notes: _____

_____

_____

Useful Feeling Words:

- Overworked, Powerless, Confused, Disillusioned, Depressed

Useful Attitudinal Words:

- Passive, Powerlessness, Down, Tired, Ashamed

My Pre-exercise Notes: _____

_____

_____

_____

_____

The suggested step for Exercise 5 is Step 1.

Exercise 6

Psalm 121:1-3

<u>Lift up Your Eyes</u>

Ps 121:1-3 - I lift up my eyes to the hills. From where does my help come? My help comes from the Lord, who made heaven and earth. He will not let your foot be moved; he who keeps you will not slumber. ESV

<u>Guiding Commentary</u> – Here the Psalmist is giving us a picture of how we ought to act, as a matter of principle, in our recovery. This is a spiritual version of "keep your chin up", meaning don't look down, but look up toward God. Looking down is what so many of us do in recovery as we are faced with the consequences of our actions, the realization of how much we have hurt others, the real nature of our character and the darkness of our sin. God says to us here, keep your chin up and look for Me! God says He will help us, He is the God of all creation and He knows how to help. He says that as we keep our gaze focused on Him, He will secure us, and that He never stops working for us in this. All we have to do is look up toward Him and accept His help.

<u>The Exercise</u> – From the moment we have been in recovery we have all experienced times of feeling down, we have felt depressed and our head has tilted downward and we have started to believe the lie, that it is not going to get better. Write about those times in your recovery when you felt despair over your situation or seeming lack of progress in becoming healed. Did you start to feel depressed, overwhelmed by life? Did you begin to doubt that God was indeed working for you, with you and in you? Consider this a personal journal of those times in recovery when you felt miserable.

Then, as a second part of this journal, write about those times when you were depressed or down that you sensed God helping you to lift your head so you could look for Him. What was the result of this in your heart, and in your attitude toward recovery and in your faith in God's ability to get you through this difficult time?

If you are in a depressed state as you do this exercise, can you lift up your eyes and look for Him? He will not force you to come to Him or look for Him; He will come to you if you do your part in getting out of a funk, and that is lifting your eyes and looking for Him. If this describes you, it might be helpful to read the story of the prodigal son (Lk 15:11-32), because it was when the prodigal lifted up his eyes and went looking for his father that the father ran to him. When one of us in recovery wants to get out of a time of despair, despondency or depression, we can lift up our eyes and look for the Father, He is waiting for us to do our part!

Sponsor Notes: _____

_____

_____

Useful Feeling Words:

- Humble, Changed, Despairing, Upset, Tempted

Useful Attitudinal Words:

- Thankful, Regretful, Depressed, Apathetic, Anxious

My Pre-exercise Notes: _____

_____

_____

_____

_____

The suggested step for Exercise 6 is Step 11.

Exercise 7

Ecclesiastes 2:1

Meaningless Pleasures

Eccl 2:1 - I said in my heart, "Come now, I will test you with pleasure; enjoy yourself." But behold, this also was vanity. **ESV**

<u>Guiding Commentary</u> – In this passage the author, thought to be Solomon, under the inspiration of the Holy Spirit writes that he has found the pleasures of this world, meaningless. Have you sought and experienced the pleasures of this world? Read Ecc 2:1-11 for a fuller picture of what this author wrote about.

<u>The Exercise</u> – After reading the passage from Ecclesiastes list the pleasures that King Solomon indulged in. Have you submerged yourself in any of these? After you have written Solomon's list, make out your own. There may be some things you have in common with the person who is reputed to be the wisest man that ever lived. Choose the three most important on your list, and describe at least 3 instances when you indulged yourself. In these spell out what you did, who was involved, when you participated in those pleasures and how you remember feeling at the time. Looking back, do you find these meaningless now, just as Solomon did? Discuss you answers with your sponsor or mentor. In your discussion identify any pleasures of this world that you are currently struggling with, and talk about how you feel after you have indulged yourself and the pleasure moment is over.

As you finalize your discussion, try to identify what behaviors or situations you are involved in that <u>do not</u> cause you to feel empty. What do you think the difference is between the old pleasures and these more recent activities? Are you experiencing joy instead of pleasure? If so, why do you think that is?

What can you do differently in your day to day life as a result of looking at pleasures through this exercise?

Sponsor Notes: _____

_____

_____

Useful Feeling Words:

- Indulging, Selfish, Ashamed, Guilty, Fearful

Useful Attitudinal Words:

- Disillusioned, Thankful, Fearful, Passive, Reluctant

My Pre-exercise Notes: _____

_____

_____

_____

_____

The suggested step for Exercise 7 is Step 4.

Exercise 8

Psalm 119:9

How Can I Stay Pure?

Ps 119:9 - How can a young man keep his way pure? By guarding it according to your word. ESV

Guiding Commentary – Psalm 119 is one of the greatest Psalms there is and it focuses on the magnificence, reliability and faithfulness of God's word. Reading the whole Psalm will give a person a picture of the God who inspired it. For those in recovery there are many golden scriptural nuggets to be mined. This one verse speaks clearly to any individual who is honestly seeking purity in his or her life. Purity, which is not perfection, but is better thought of as not being stained or contaminated by sin, is found by simply obeying God's word. There is no other guide that has ever been written that can lead a person into purity. (One might also look at Phil 4:8-9 to obtain a New Testament view of how important purity is in a person's life.)

Most people in recovery recognize that they have led an impure life, even those that don't believe in the one true God. After recognizing that we cannot manage some parts of our lives and that we are powerless over our compulsions and addictions in step one, we come to a new choice in step two. Recognizing that there is one who can help restore our sanity, which can also be thought of as mental purity, and His name is Jesus.

The Exercise – This exercise might take a little work! Identify at least three ways you have led an impure life, three behaviors that could be said to be insanity in operation in your life. Then comb through scripture to track down three scriptural passages that speak about each one of these impurities in our actions. These passages could be stories (King David's life is often a good source for that!) or commands or instructions. Then for each of the three behaviors you listed write down some of the typical thoughts and feelings you might have been having before you acted out. Also attempt to identify the attitudinal states you might have been in during your times of impurity. (Examples might be "I was lonely" or "I was depressed")

As you look at the results of your work are you connecting the dots here? Do you see how our attitudinal states, and our thoughts and feelings during those times directed us toward actions that scripturally speaking were impure, which then led to negative consequences? Can you also then see how, when your difficult attitudinal states and troublesome emotions or thoughts, were never actually changed through personal application of scriptural principles you continued to act out?

Our focus scripture above says that purity, and as applied here, mental purity or sanity, is found in following God's ways. Knowing this, can you come up with your own definition of sanity using this scripture as a guide?

Sponsor Notes: _____

_____

_____

Useful Feeling Words:

- Unclean, Troubled, Sincere, Grateful, Down

Useful Attitudinal Words:

- Denial, Depressed, Anxious, Rebelliousness, Joyless

My Pre-exercise Notes: _____

_____

_____

_____

_____

The suggested step for Exercise 8 is Step 2.

Exercise 9

Ecclesiastes 8:8

<u>Wickedness Binds</u>

Eccl 8:8 - No man has power to retain the spirit, or power over the day of death. There is no discharge from war, nor will wickedness deliver those who are given to it. ESV

<u>Guiding Commentary</u> - In this one verse we see some timeless truths. It starts with the truth that no one can contain the spirit (called wind in some translations), and compares that to the truth that none of us know when we are going to die. It is the second part of this verse that we are going to address in this exercise. This says that just as a soldier is kept in the army in wartime, none of us can be freed from our wickedness, meaning the behaviors and sins that trap us. We are asked by God to compare the reality that when a war is going on, those in the armed forces have to continue to serve, with the reality that we are trapped by our compulsions and addictions. (We can acknowledge that in modern day western style armed forces this reality is not strongly applied, but it still is in other parts of the world, and was true back in ancient times.) In the armed forces, the rule of law is set by the powers in charge, a combination of political government and generals. In our addictions or compulsions the rule of law is still present. It is the law of sin, which says something like this "I have got you under my control, your life is hopeless, and you are powerless to control it, and I am ruling you." Our scripture says it something like this, "Wickedness will not release those who practice it."

<u>The Exercise</u> – Write out a description of how you have been bound up by sin. Start by identifying the behavioral aspects of your most grievous sin by writing out what you have done in a general sense. This might be one paragraph. Then write one paragraph each, giving actual examples, on how you were powerless over it, how you tried to manage it and couldn't, and finally how and when you came to realize that you felt hopeless. In talking about your powerlessness, describe and name the feelings that you experienced or maybe still do. By now you will have at least four paragraphs written.

The next part of this exercise is to try to identify what emotional state you might have been in, or maybe are still in, that contributed to you surrendering to sin so easily. Write out what you perceive as your probable thoughts and feelings that went with these emotional states. Add any words you can think of that might describe the impulsive nature of how you moved from an emotional state into acting out.

Finally, write one paragraph describing how you felt, or still feel, bound up by your sin. Use some of these key words; chains, ropes, restraints, shackles, immobilized, fastened down, trapped, bound up or any similar words that come to you.

Sponsor Notes: _____

_____

_____

Useful Feeling Words:

- Powerless, Hopeless, Guilty, Ashamed, Down

Useful Attitudinal Words:

- Hurting, Powerlessness, Medicated, Unfeeling, Depressed

My Pre-exercise Notes: _____

_____

_____

_____

The suggested step for Exercise 9 is Step 1.

Exercise 10

Proverbs 4:23

<u>Guard the Heart</u>

Prov 4:23 - Keep your heart with all vigilance, for from it flow the springs of life. ESV

<u>Guiding Commentary</u> –.This is part of a section of scripture, Proverbs chapter 4, which covers the subject of the supremacy of God's wisdom. Throughout the Bible we see godly wisdom extolled and earthly wisdom warned against. Chapter 4 of Proverbs refers to godly wisdom, and this verse may be the most important of them all. It speaks to us from the heart of the Father saying, "If there is one thing you must remember about wisdom this is it." So, we all ought to pay attention to what God is about to tell us! He says to **guard our hearts**, not our minds, or any other part of us; it is the heart that must be protected above all other things. And then He tells us why, "It is the wellspring of life." This word "wellspring" signifies that the heart is the source, fountain and origin of everything about us. This scripture admonishes us to protect it from corruption, pollution and any other form of ungodly influence, because whatever we let into it will in turn influence our lives.

<u>The Exercise</u> – You'll need a Bible to complete this exercise.

Write out the first part of Romans 10:10. Now explain how this statement fits in with our focus verse above. Then write out your personal assessment about what you must have believed when you were acting out, or if you still are acting out, write out what your behaviors indicate you believe. Try to list three false (ungodly) beliefs that you had (have) and what they have been replaced by if you have worked to eliminate them from your heart.

Now, read Eph 6:10-18. Identify and write out what the six pieces of armor are. In verse 14(b) it lists an item, the breastplate of righteousness, what part of the anatomy of a soldier was a breastplate protecting? Write out your thoughts on why God calls this the "Breastplate of Righteousness" and not something else. Focus on what "righteousness" means in our everyday lives.

Finally, describe what righteousness looks like in your life, and spell out the benefits to your heart, and to the people you love, of putting on the breastplate of righteousness.

Sponsor Notes: _____

_____

_____

Useful Feeling Words:

- Attacked, Tempted, Unsafe, Guilty, Unprotected

Useful Attitudinal Words:

- Vulnerable, Nervous, Frustrated, Despairing, Powerlessness

My Pre-exercise Notes: _____

_____

_____

_____

_____

The suggested step for Exercise 10 is Step 11.

Exercise 11

Psalm 138:1-3

<u>Have You Called God?</u>

Ps 138:1-3 - I give you thanks, O Lord, with my whole heart; before the gods I sing your praise; I bow down toward your holy temple and give thanks to your name for your steadfast love and your faithfulness, for you have exalted above all things your name and your word. On the day I called, you answered me; my strength of soul you increased. ESV

<u>Guiding Commentary</u> – There is a powerful message here for those of us in recovery. One can simply read this and see another straightforward spiritual message. Or one can look at this with the eyes of a person recovering from the tyranny of a compulsion or addiction. No matter what stage we might be at in our recovery this message can resonate in our souls. Understanding this scripture starts with realizing that our "problem" can be looked at as an idol in our lives, something we worship and make the object of our faith. It might seem strange to see gambling or sex or money or work as objects of faith, however as we ponder this we can see that we rely on our "acting out" to make us feel better, meaning we have faith in these compulsions or addictions to help us in some way. In this scripture we can see that we are being encouraged to praise the One True God even as we are facing the idols, called "gods" in this scripture, through temptation to act out again. Then in that last sentence we are told that when we call on Him, He will answer by providing us with the courage to resist the temptation to fall into our idol worship once again.

<u>The Exercise</u> – Take time to write out a description of what the "gods" of your life have been; include those you may be struggling with still. Take the three you consider the most significant in your life and for each of them try to capture in written words what need(s) or desire(s) in your life was operating inside of you such that you were electing to idolize them. Then, in writing, admit to God that you put these things before Him, and ask Him in this personal written prayer to forgive you of this, in accordance with 1 Jn 1:9.

For those who have been in recovery for a while – have your idols changed since your early days? Write out a paragraph about this, and remembering that denial is a big barrier to the truth, you might want to ask someone who knows you well, such as a sponsor or mentor, to help you think this through. Then move on to writing out the answer to this question, "Are you still struggling with those same needs or desires mentioned in the first part of this exercise?"

Finally, make a written commitment to God, to one trusted person and to yourself that the next time you face your idols, you will "call" on Him to give you strength to beat them back.

Sponsor Notes: _____

_____

_____

Useful Feeling Words:

- Weak, Misled, Thankful, Guilty, Purposeless

Useful Attitudinal Words:

- Powerlessness, Rebelliousness, Drifting, Uncaring, Disillusioned

My Pre-exercise Notes: _____

_____

_____

_____

_____

The suggested step for Exercise 11 is Step 7.

Exercise 12

Proverbs 29:6

Evil Snares!

Prov 29:6 - An evil man is ensnared in his transgression, but a righteous man sings and rejoices. ESV

<u>Guiding Commentary</u> – This is another one of those explicit comparisons found in Proverbs. Here we see the comparison of an evil heart with a righteous one and the product of each. The person with an evil heart will be trapped by their own sin, whereas the person with a heart that seeks to live right will sing and experience gladness.

The Christian position on the nature of people rests on a simple premise. Every person is evil, and some, even within the church have trouble believing this. So to make sure you see where this truth comes from read Ps 14:3, Isa 53:6 and Rom 3:23.

<u>The Exercise</u> – Have you ever considered that you were born evil? Look back on your life and write out a short description of some of the sins you have committed that you know about. List at least 10 specific sins, and state who you hurt as a result of these, which will most likely include yourself. At the end of this list write out a simple statement of confession that declares that you know and agree with God that you were evil during these times, that you still have a propensity to be evil and that you need God to help you overcome this propensity on a daily basis.

Now, to provide balance, list ten things you have done that were "the right thing to do" or righteous in nature. As you do this, list the people who benefitted from it. If you are in recovery, the righteous act of being in Christ-centered recovery ought to be first on the list. If you are merely in recovery, you cannot list it as it is not righteous in nature, it is self-centered. If you don't understand the difference, speak with your Christian sponsor.

As you consider both lists, would you say that your life proves this proverb to be true? Write out a statement about this for your permanent recovery file for your use later.

Sponsor Notes: _____

_____

_____

Useful Feeling Words:

- Hoodwinked, Deceived, Blind, Upset, Humbled

Useful Attitudinal Words:

- Humility, Honesty, Dark-minded, Freed, Released

My Pre-exercise Notes: _____

_____

_____

_____

_____

The suggested step for Exercise 12 is Step 4.

Exercise 13

Proverbs 16:25

<u>I Did it My Way</u>

Prov 16:25 - There is a way that seems right to a man, but its end is the way to death. ESV

<u>Guiding Commentary</u> – Whenever I look at this verse I almost always end up thinking about Frank Sinatra singing his most famous song, "My Way." In this song he proudly proclaims that he did it all his way. The problem is he forgot the second half of the story, that he ran over people, hurt them and possibly worst of all most likely ended up in Hell (which we don't know for sure, because we don't know if he ever accepted Jesus).

For those of us in recovery this verse may not need to be explained. We have, for the most part, realized that our best thinking got us into a bad place, and for some of us that became a living death. Some of us ended up losing everything, living out of our cars or on the streets, alone, hungry, broken and in a state of hopelessness. And for those of us who reached a "bottom" we would probably say that it felt like a death.

So for this exercise, we are going to assume that we mostly understand this, and we'll therefore look at what it is inside that causes us to believe that our way is "right."

<u>The Exercise</u> – For this exercise we want to take a look at what is inside us that drives us to make so many unhealthy choices. Let's begin with confessing some things. Write out a simple list of your core beliefs, values and attitudes; limit yourself to five of each. In doing this do not include any item that is cliché in nature such as "love of family" or "I believe in God" for these are protective statements that indicate you are wearing an "emotional mask."

What you ought to see on your list are things like, "I know what it right for me" or "Resentfulness of others" and we would expect every person to list "pride in self" as a core value. It is often helpful to ask others we trust to help us produce such a list for others can see things in us that we are blind to.

28

Now prioritize your personal list and for the top three of each write out a one paragraph description of some event from your acting out days where this belief, value or attitude was demonstrated, and what the result was.

Finally write out a one paragraph statement confessing any lingering ways that you hang on to these damaging beliefs, values and attitudes. Consider this as your prayer to God for help with these character defects.

Sponsor Notes: _____

_____

_____

Useful Feeling Words:

- Afraid, Proud, Arrogant, Nervous, Anxious

Useful Attitudinal Words:

- Rebelliousness, Disobedient, Selfish, Uncaring, Prideful

My Pre-exercise Notes: _____

_____

_____

_____

_____

The suggested step for Exercise 13 is Step 4.

Exercise 14

Ecclesiastes 2:10-11

<u>Gaining Nothing</u>

Eccl 2:10-11 - Whatever my eyes desired I did not keep from them. I kept my heart from no pleasure, for my heart found pleasure in all my toil, and this was my reward for all my toil. Then I considered all that my hands had done and the toil I had expended in doing it, and behold, all was vanity and a striving after wind, and there was nothing to be gained under the sun. ESV

<u>Guiding Commentary</u> – In this scripture we see the author, Solomon, declare that he denied his eyes nothing and his heart no pleasure. In modern words he had everything his heart or eyes lusted after, he never said "no" to anything that he wanted. If he wanted sex, he had it, if it was booze, he had it, money he had it, power and fame he had it. He was a workaholic too! And in the end, in the last days of his life he penned these words, "I looked at it all, and it was all meaningless, I had gained nothing!"

Even though it was Solomon who wrote these words down, we must remember that he was under the guidance of the Holy Spirit, meaning that these are God approved words containing a message for us, something for us to ponder over. Here the message is that our pleasures, the things we get involved in to feel better, and our works, the things we do to feel better are all of no use to us.

<u>The Exercise</u> – Write a list of the pleasures you've pursued, and a list of the works you have done. List only those things you've done believing you'll get some kind of emotional payback. For this exercise assume emotional payback is that one feels better about oneself, or about life in general, even if those feelings didn't persist. An example would be a gambler who takes a risk, then feels better when one pays off through a winning hand, even though the feeling is gone in a short time. Take the top three pleasures and the top three works and write out a paragraph on each detailing why you believe you got involved in them, what need or want you might have been trying to satisfy, the emotional result at the time you engaged in them and how you feel about them now.

(Examples of pleasures might be sex, alcohol, drugs, gambling, golfing and people pleasing; works could be keeping the house clean, playing sports, coaching little league, teaching bible studies, running for political office et.)

After this is completed, write a short summary of how you feel about all of these things from your past, stating if you agree with Solomon, and expanding on why or why not.

Sponsor Notes: _____

_____

_____

Useful Feeling Words:

- Pleasure, Concerned, Afraid, Ashamed, Guilty

Useful Attitudinal Words:

- Rebellious, Obstinate, Prideful, Ignorant, Evasive

My Pre-exercise Notes: _____

_____

_____

_____

_____

The suggested step for Exercise 14 is Step 10.

Exercise 15

Psalm 37:21

<u>Wicked or Righteous?</u>

Ps 37:21 - The wicked borrows but does not pay back, but the righteous is generous and gives. ESV

<u>Guiding Commentary</u> – Psalm 37 is about trusting in God and doing things His way. Parts of it, such as our focus verse, contrast those that trust in God and demonstrate it through obedience and those that don't. Here the two are categorized as righteous or wicked. Don't get hung up on these two words too much as we are going to apply this to the results of recovery.

One of the hallmarks of a person achieving healing through recovery work, which in the context of our verse is described as becoming right with God (righteous), is that they want to give back. They want to give back generously by telling their story, by serving God in the lives of others in recovery, and by giving some of their material resources to assist God's work in Christ-centered recovery. Most importantly they do this from an attitude of gratefulness. In twelve step groups, these are the people who are consistently working Step 12.

In contrast we see someone who might be in recovery, but operates by taking the help and other resources given by the generous ones, but doesn't contribute to God's work in any way. They are the borrowers and takers, the users, who are still stuck in their negative emotional states, and who are most likely experiencing relief from their problems, but not healing. Our scripture calls these people wicked. This may sound strong, but when we look at those around us that take and don't give back, is there a better word to describe them?

<u>The Exercise</u> – Think back to the time you entered recovery. Write out what state you were in using the context of the guiding commentary above. Were you feeling generous or were you simply taking whatever was offered you? Did you come into your recovery fellowship feeling righteous or wicked? Were you a taker and a user, or were you a giver? Write about the state of your inner self, was it in a state of "I'm entitled to help" so you took things that were offered as "freebies" or were

you taking because "I'm desperate for help"; maybe you have some other words you would prefer to use.

Next think about how things are now, and write about it. Tell yourself and your guide, sponsor or mentor the state of your inner person today. Are you carrying an attitude of generosity or thankfulness, and if you are, how do you show it? Spell out what you are thankful for, and who you are thankful to; name names, give credit to whomever you believe has helped you. Give glory to God if you believe that is appropriate.

Sponsor Notes: _____

_____

_____

Useful Feeling Words:

- Prideful, Ashamed, Glad, Empowered, Vulnerable

Useful Attitudinal Words:

- Prideful, Selfish, Rebellious, Tight-fisted, Hard-Hearted

My Pre-exercise Notes: _____

_____

_____

_____

_____

The suggested step for Exercise 15 is Step 6.

Exercise 16

Proverbs 14:9

<u>Taking Amends Seriously</u>

Prov 14:9 - Fools mock at the guilt offering, but the upright enjoy acceptance. ESV

<u>Guiding Commentary</u> – Fools, folly and foolishness are words found throughout the Bible, and are mentioned extensively in Proverbs. In our culture a fool is nothing more than a person who lives or acts in ignorance, or maybe an unintelligent or ridiculous person, or a person that lacks good judgment. The fool of the Bible is defined differently. There are three words we translate as fool; peti (simple one), kesil (dullard) and ewil (mocker of sin). You will not be surprised that the third word is the one used in our verse and is the source of our English word "evil."

For our purposes then, as people in Christ-centered recovery, we must realize this verse tells us that it is an act of evil to not make amends for sin. This is entirely consistent with the concepts of repentance and restitution found throughout the Bible. Our willingness, or lack of it, to make amends is therefore an indicator of the state of our heart. Even though it is not explicit in our verse, we are instructed by God to be willing to make amends, so that to not be willing is mocking Him. This of course doesn't mean we will be able, mostly due to circumstances, to make amends to every person on our list, we are just asked to be persons of "goodwill" through this verse.

<u>The Exercise</u> – Describe in writing the beliefs, values and attitudes you may have had when you first encountered the reality that you had to make face to face amends. Then add a description of the thoughts and emotions that sprang up inside you when this problem of having to make amends to other people you had harmed came up. Words like fear, trepidation, unnecessary, no, anxiety, expensive, revenge and resentful may be part of your written dialogue.

In the light of what this verse says do you consider yourself as having been a "fool" when you first realized what amend-making meant? Do you connect with this as a state of evil that existed inside you at that time? Confess this to God in a prayer, in accordance with 1 Jn 1:9.

Having been through some basic recovery work, do you now consider making amends a necessity for you, or are you still struggling with it? Write about this.

Finally, sit down with your most significant godly advisor and discuss the subject of having an evil, commonly called sinful, nature. Address with him or her the changes in your beliefs, values and attitudes you have experienced inside as you have worked through some recovery, and how these changes are lessening the evil nature, and how you are becoming less and less a "fool."

Sponsor Notes: _____

_____

_____

Useful Feeling Words:

- Unworthy, Ashamed, Humiliated, Fearful, Vulnerable

Useful Attitudinal Words:

- Rebellious, Disobedient, Foolishness, Denial, Mocking

My Pre-exercise Notes: _____

_____

_____

_____

_____

The suggested step for Exercise 16 is Step 8.

Exercise 17

Psalms 86:11

<u>Teach Me</u>

Ps 86:11 - Teach me your way, O Lord, that I may walk in your truth; unite my heart to fear your name. ESV

<u>Guiding Commentary</u> – In this verse we see, as we do in other places in scripture, the writer asking God to be taught in His ways. The writer of this prayer psalm is promising to walk in God's truth and he deeply desires to have an undivided heart so that he may fear the Lord. For some extra context we must also remember that "fear of the Lord" is described in scripture as the beginning of wisdom. For us in recovery this speaks to the understanding that it was our best thinking that got us into trouble, so maybe asking the Lord to help us with this through learning better ways of doing life isn't such a bad idea.

Our question here is, "Do you have a teachable heart?" This is actually a question that every sponsor, mentor or therapist ought to ask us as we enter into the phase of recovery where we want to get better. In the twelve steps this might be Step 3; it could also be applied daily in our lives through Step 11.

For the purposes of this exercise, a teachable heart is one that first realizes that it is sick (Jer 17:9), then acknowledges that it cannot help itself and finally realizes that God is the only one who can. This is what David, the psalmist, was expressing in our focus verse. God in His infinite wisdom has given us three resources to use to help us with our sick heart; His Word, His Spirit and His Church.

<u>The Exercise</u> – For the first part of this exercise, write out a statement that describes the state of your heart before you entered recovery. List some examples of your behaviors that demonstrated this. Next list some of the barriers that existed in your heart to being teachable, understanding that if you say you were always teachable, or that there were only minor barriers, you are living in denial, and you may want to speak with a godly advisor about it.

Assuming you are in full agreement with God about the state of your heart, write out a prayer for yourself that lines up with our scripture. In this prayer, begin by acknowledging God; who and what He is to you. Then move to confessing that you have a sick heart, listing out some of the sicknesses you know about. Next, place yourself under His wing by asking for His help, first in being able to put aside your ungodly beliefs, values and attitudes, then in being able to see what He has for you in His word, in your prayer life through conversation with Him and through the godly people in your life. Finally add some words of pleading to God to help you be truly teachable by Him, through His word and His people. Pray this each day for a week, then share and discuss it with your sponsor, mentor, therapist or other godly advisor.

Sponsor Notes: _____

_____

_____

Useful Feeling Words:

- Sick, Hurt, Fearful, Ignorant, Enlightened

Useful Attitudinal Words:

- Denial, Hiding, Escapism, Prideful, Embarrassment

My Pre-exercise Notes: _____

_____

_____

_____

The suggested step for Exercise 17 is Step 3.

Exercise 18

Ecclesiastes 3:1

Time for Recovery

Eccl 3:1 - For everything there is a season, and a time for every matter under heaven. ESV

Guiding Commentary – This is a part of the well known "time for" piece of scripture (Eccl 3:1-8) which has been used in so many speeches and songs over the years. Take a moment to read it through.

In this verse God is speaking out to tell us something we all know; there is a time for everything. This is so true for us in Christian recovery. There is time to stop doing the things we began so many years ago, a time to admit our transgressions to God, a time to confess our sins to one another and a time to begin serious recovery.

Interestingly, Christian recovery does not begin with some form of confession of our sins. Instead it begins with an acknowledgement of some fundamental truths. We must acknowledge that we are powerless over our issue, that we are helpless, having no ability to overcome the issue(s), and that we cannot manage that part of our life. This is true for all forms of recovery, Christian or not.

In this exercise we are going to shine a light on what this acknowledgement looks like for us in our individual situations.

The Exercise – Write out a statement of your personal beliefs and thoughts on the three fundamental truths in three short paragraphs. Begin each paragraph with an "I am" statement; for example "I am powerless over _____ because………".

Now construct another paragraph discussing what your latest recovery bottom looks and feels like in the context of the three truths of powerlessness, helplessness and unmanageability.

Finally write out a prayer for yourself, asking God to reveal anything you may have missed in your work. Pray this for yourself, and if you are comfortable with doing this ask others to pray it for you. Then add an addendum of what was revealed, without changing the original work you've done.

After this is complete, take it to your next regularly scheduled meeting for discussion with your sponsor, counselor or mentor.

Sponsor Notes: _____

_____

_____

Useful Feeling Words:

- Confused, Guilty, Exposed, Powerless, Unworthy

Useful Attitudinal Words:

- Disillusioned, Apathetic, Detached, Hopelessness, Denial

My Pre-exercise Notes: _____

_____

_____

_____

_____

The suggested step for Exercise 18 is Step 1.

Exercise 19

Proverbs 15:22

A Component of Victory

Prov 15:22 - Without counsel plans fail, but with many advisers they succeed. ESV

Guiding Commentary – Some of us who have been operating in the field of recovery for a while believe it is wise for an individual to develop a written recovery plan. This is because we have the view that we are in a personal war and we are not well equipped to fight it by ourselves. In this verse we see a principle, a basic truth, that without advisors the most likely outcome of our recovery work is failure. It has been said that people don't plan to fail, they fail to plan. This is something that is worth thinking about in the context of recovery. In our context here failure is getting some relief from our troubles, but not healing; failure is having trouble remaining completely sober; failure is experiencing slips and relapses and failure is dismissing recovery as ineffective. Here are some things to consider:

- We are basically ignorant coming into recovery. This ensures that a self-made, self-written plan, or no plan, will result in failure.
- We have serious character issues or defects, which cause us to be blind to the truth that experienced recovery individuals can easily see.
- Not writing a plan down means we have not established accountability standards to measure progress by, so we are basically unaccountable.
- We are in a spiritual war, where we are our own biggest enemy.
- We need experienced individuals to come alongside us to guide and counsel us through the whole process of recovery.

The help of others in building a personal recovery plan, in executing it and in reforming it from time to time is the surest component to success in recovery that there is.

The Exercise – Do you agree with this or not? Write out why.

Do you have a written recovery plan? If yes, did you write it yourself or did someone else help you? What does it say? Write out your answer, describing the process of forming the plan, what help you got and its major highlights. If no, why not? Write out why you don't have a plan. Look for barriers inside your beliefs, values and attitudes that are preventing you from seeking help from others. Are you being rebellious toward God in this matter?

Finally, list the names of at least five advisors that you use in your recovery work, whether you have a plan or not, and do not include spouses on this list. State their role and how often you consult with them.

Sponsor Notes: _____

_____

_____

Useful Feeling Words:

- Scared, Pain, Fearful, Ashamed, Rejected

Useful Attitudinal Words:

- Gratitude, Rebelliousness, Prideful, Vulnerable, Anxiety

My Pre-exercise Notes: _____

_____

_____

_____

The suggested step for Exercise 19 is Step 5.

Exercise 20

Proverbs 14:21

Helping the Needy

Prov 14:21 - Whoever despises his neighbor is a sinner, but blessed is he who is generous to the poor. ESV

Guiding Commentary – This is the kind of Proverb that we can all easily connect with on a general social level. In this exercise though, we are going to consider it in the context of recovery. First let's be clear on who our "neighbor" is and who the "needy" are in recovery. Our neighbor is any person in our immediate recovery groups, fellowships or related organizations. (If we were talking about AA for example, it would include every member of AA worldwide) We are neighbors, not by geography, but by behavioral category. The "needy" are all those members of our neighbor groups who come behind us in recovery, this would mostly be the "newbies" and the less mature, recovery wise.

God says that we are NOT to "despise" our neighbor. Recovery groups are like any other group, some of us simply do not get along, we let differences of opinion get in the way of the common good, and end up disliking or even despising the very people who we should get along with best. God calls this a sin.

More importantly, God encourages us to be kind to the needy. In recovery this refers mostly to the immature, ignorant and hurting among us. We are nudged into doing whatever it takes to move these people from their difficult emotional states to places of knowledge about recovery, and to feelings of hope and courage in facing their troubles. In short, we are to give back to our neighborhood (our groups) what has been given to us in the past by those that went before us. And as an extra benefit, God promises that we will be blessed.

The Exercise – How are you doing with helping the needy? Write a description of the talents you have and how you are using them to support your recovery fellowship. In the next paragraph, specifically detail the actions you perform, and how much time you give each week to the smooth running of the group or assisting other group members at a more personal level. In a third paragraph, speak to the things you give to the group that can be quantified, such as time and money.

Finally make a statement about how satisfied you are with your contributions to the group(s) you attend.

For the second part of this exercise respond to these statements. "People who are not grateful for what God has done for them in recovery demonstrate it by not giving back to God; this is an external indicator of their internal spiritual condition and that they have not taken recovery seriously and have not received the healing that they could. They are likely to fall away from the fellowship of recovery and eventually relapse."

Sponsor Notes: _____

_____

_____

Useful Feeling Words:

- Satisfied, Triumphant, Encouraged, Alive, Challenged

Useful Attitudinal Words:

- Contentment, Victorious, Courageous, Prideful, Spiritual

My Pre-exercise Notes: _____

_____

_____

_____

_____

The suggested step for Exercise 20 is Step 6.

Exercise 21

Psalms 111:7-10

<u>Believe God?</u>

Ps 111:7-10 - The works of his hands are faithful and just; all his precepts are trustworthy; they are established forever and ever, to be performed with faithfulness and uprightness. He sent redemption to his people; he has commanded his covenant forever. Holy and awesome is his name! The fear of the Lord is the beginning of wisdom; all those who practice it have a good understanding. His praise endures forever! ESV

<u>Guiding Commentary</u> – This is one of many declarations in scripture about the One True God. Look at what this Psalm says about Him. He created it all, and we can rely on the physical realm to operate according to the way it designed (*faithful and just*), His laws are *trustworthy*. Those laws can be relied on as they were created within God's *faithfulness and uprightness*, out of who He is. He provided us with *redemption* (In Jesus!) he declared His predetermined *covenant*. His name is the only name that is *holy and awesome*. The *fear of the Lord* is a smart thing to have as it leads to *wisdom and understanding* as we follow His *precepts* (laws and instructions). To Him be everlasting praise.

In reading and reflecting on what this Psalm declares the big question is not, "do you believe in God?" It is "do you believe God?"

In this exercise we want to challenge our beliefs, because it is out of our beliefs that we will act, and we also know that our actions reveal our beliefs.

<u>The Exercise</u> – First go back to a time before you entered recovery. Write down up to five primary activities that you engaged in, examples could be "controlling others" or "drink too much" or "viewed porn" or "worked excessively." For each of these explain the extent you engaged in them and the effects of them on you and the people around you. Then for each of them write out if they demonstrated belief in God and His precepts (his laws and instructions). For the final part of this exercise write out how you feel about this.

Now, look at five primary activities you engage in today (they may be different) and list them, then write out what you think they reveal about the extent of whether you believe God or not.

Sponsor Notes: _____

_____

_____

Useful Feeling Words:

- Ashamed, Guilty, Contempt, Unworthy, Lost

Useful Attitudinal Words:

- Resentment, Prideful, Disobedient, Burdened, Worthlessness

My Pre-exercise Notes: _____

_____

_____

_____

_____

The suggested step for Exercise 21 is Step 2.

Exercise 22

Proverbs 18:1

An Enemy Called Isolation

Prov 18:1 - Whoever isolates himself seeks his own desire; he breaks out against all sound judgment. ESV

Guiding Commentary – The scripture above is from our standard text, the ESV. Another useful translation is found here from the Amplified Bible:

Prov 18:1 - HE WHO willfully separates and estranges himself [from God and man] seeks his own desire and pretext to break out against all wise and sound judgment. AMP

When we look at this we can see some clear insight into human nature. When we isolate, which is to *separate and estrange ourselves*, we are seeking our own selfish desires. And when we do that we are *"breaking out against all wise and sound judgment."*

Those of us with some recovery experience recognize that isolating is something we have all done. Here are some truths about isolation:

- It is always an emotional and spiritual separation from others, including God.
- It may also include a physical separation.
- We are often unconscious of our isolation.
- We think that being a loner is normal, and is the way things are.
- Isolation always leads to immoral choices.

The Exercise – Go back to when you were "acting out" and not in recovery in a committed and serious way. Write out a description of five acting out events. For each of these five events list the names of five or six key adults in your life at that time, and say if they knew what you were doing or not., and if they did, if they encouraged you to "act out." Having done this, next address this question, "Do these five events demonstrate a fit with the five truths listed above?"

Isolation is usually a very important component of a person's acting out story. Having looked back, let us now look at today. Write out a short statement about if and how you isolate in your life.

Finally write out a plan, containing specific action you are going to take, of how you are going to avoid isolation for the rest of your life. Start your plan with these words. "Because I isolate, and isolation is my enemy, I am writing this plan to deal with it in my present and future life." You may want to confer with a couple of recovery-oriented godly advisors as you develop your plan.

Sponsor Notes: _____

_____

_____

Useful Feeling Words:

- Isolated, Rejected, Worthless, Angry, Ashamed

Useful Attitudinal Words:

- Resentments, Bitterness, Hopelessness, Joylessness, Pain

My Pre-exercise Notes: _____

_____

_____

_____

_____

The suggested step for Exercise 22 is Step 1.

Exercise 23

Psalms 88:3-5

<u>Cut Off From God</u>

Ps 88:3-5 - For my soul is full of troubles, and my life draws near to Sheol. I am counted among those who go down to the pit; I am a man who has no strength, like one set loose among the dead, like the slain that lie in the grave, like those whom you remember no more, for they are cut off from your hand. ESV

<u>Guiding Commentary</u> – This was written by someone who was most likely experiencing what we call in recovery, "a bottom." Look at what he says and see if you connect with it as I paraphrase the verses.

- My soul is full of trouble, and I feel like I'm about to die. I'm a member of the walking dead who are headed for Hell, I'm miserable, I have no strength or power, and I can't help myself. I'm alone like a dead person who is lying in the grave. And God, you've forgotten about me, like you don't care about me anymore, if you ever did!

Strong words! Most of us in recovery have experienced these kinds of emotional states. The twelve steps call them powerlessness and hopelessness.

<u>The Exercise</u> – When you read this, do you remember what it felt like when you were in your darkest pit? Write about it; describe the event or events that led you into this place of hopelessness. In your own words express what you were feeling at this time; were you ready to give up on something, maybe your marriage, or your relationship with God, or even your own life?

For the next part of this exercise, write about what it took to get you from your bottom to reaching out to a counselor or a recovery group. As you detail this, be sure to recognize who was involved in helping you. If you named God as one who helped, write out a short prayer of thanks to Him, spelling out what you believe He did for you.

Finally, what would you say to someone who came to you expressing themselves the way this Psalmist did?

Sponsor Notes: _____

_____

_____

Useful Feeling Words:

- Powerless, Hopeless, Unworthy, Forgotten, Damaged

Useful Attitudinal Words:

- Laziness, Blaming, Hopelessness, Victimhood, Irresponsibility

My Pre-exercise Notes: _____

_____

_____

_____

_____

The suggested step for Exercise 23 is Step 1.

Exercise 24

Psalms 144:3-4

<u>Life is Short</u>

Ps 144:3-4 - O Lord, what is man that you regard him, or the son of man that you think of him? Man is like a breath; his days are like a passing shadow. ESV

<u>Guiding Commentary</u> – This is one of those reflective passages that God has put into scripture to help us to think about ourselves in relationship to Him correctly. Here the Psalmist declares, under God's guidance something like this:

- Why do you think of us humans, God, and care for us the way you do? We are nothing, here today and gone tomorrow, just like a shadow that flits through the day.

God wants us to think about the fact that, in the eternal perspective, life is short. He wants us to fill our lives with Him as much as He fills His time with us.

In the context of recovery, we can apply this to the realization that we have spent our limited life chasing lusts; lust of the eyes, lust of the flesh and the boastful pride of life (see 1 Jn 2:16). Our time will come to an end soon, and we will have wasted it, and yet God still cares for us!

<u>The Exercise</u> – Find a Bible, an ESV if possible. Look up and read 1 John 2:15-17. Now write it out, and add one word in front of it, your first name. After this, reread it as a personal message from God to you.

Now write out your own paraphrase of the focus verse of this exercise with you as the object. Be sure to identify the key points; that you are seemingly insignificant, that God cares for and thinks about you all the time, that you are just as a single breath, taken and gone; and you are like a shadow that passes quickly.

Finally write out a prayer response to whatever God has put in your mind and heart during this exercise.

Sponsor Notes: _____

_____

_____

Useful Feeling Words:

- Lustful, Shame, Guilt, Insignificant, Unworthy

Useful Attitudinal Words:

- Worthlessness, Inadequacy, Bitterness, Inability, Withdrawn

My Pre-exercise Notes: _____

_____

_____

_____

_____

The suggested step for Exercise 24 is Step 10.

Exercise 25

Psalms 29:1

<u>Stiff Necked Relapse</u>

Prov 29:1 - He who is often reproved, yet stiffens his neck, will suddenly be broken beyond healing. ESV

<u>Guiding Commentary</u> – One interesting way of looking at recovery is to consider it a series of chastisements or rebukes. In recovery some things about our behaviors and thinking are exposed as being immoral, sinful or just plain wrong and we experience these as criticisms or condemnation even though they are rarely that. This scripture identifies one common response we see from some who begin recovery, they become "stiff necked." This often comes out as rejection of the messages of recovery, not because they are invalid or inaccurate, but because the receiver has certain attitudes.

Rejection of recovery messages is often done from an attitude of rebelliousness. This attitude has its roots in pride, this pride causes some individuals to internally respond like this; "no one is telling me what to do." Thus they become stiff-necked.

Our proverb assures us that if we continue to reject God's recovery messages and become stiff-necked, he will either lift His protective hand from us, or introduce some form of discipline into our lives, such that we are likely to be destroyed, and destroyed so that we cannot recover from whatever befalls us.

We have called being stiff-necked a relapse, not because it is a repeat of a compulsive behavior, but because it is a repeat of bad thinking due to bad and ungodly attitudes.

<u>The Exercise</u> – Spend some time meditating on how you respond or react to recovery messages. These messages come to you from three main sources; scripture, the Holy Spirit and believers (meaning your recovery groups). Messages may also be sourced from the world, where the Holy Spirit takes a worldly message and adapts it for you. Do you sense an attitude of rebellion, or maybe laziness or entitlement?

Write about at least two incidents where you were stiff-necked toward your recovery. What do these two incidents tell you about yourself, about your relationship with God and how well you accept and submit to those who are trying to help you?

Does the thought of losing it all, and falling back into a relapse scare you? Document your fear or lack of fear for your sponsor or counselor to discuss with you.

Sponsor Notes: _____

_____

_____

Useful Feeling Words:

- Sorry, Regret, Disciplined Ashamed, Guilty

Useful Attitudinal Words:

- Helplessness, Powerlessness, Brokenness, Resentment, Lost

My Pre-exercise Notes: _____

_____

_____

_____

_____

The suggested step for Exercise 25 is Step 6.

Exercise 26

Ecclesiastes 7:3

Seeking Sorrow

Eccl 7:3 - Sorrow is better than laughter, for by sadness of face the heart is made glad. ESV

Guiding Commentary – It might seem a little bizarre that God says that sorrow is better than laughter, that is until you read the second part of the verse. There it tells us that our sorrow (sad face) is good for the heart. Why is this? Here are the big clues:

2 Cor 7:10 - Godly sorrow brings repentance that leads to salvation and leaves no regret. NIV

2 Cor 7:11 -See what this godly sorrow has produced in you: what earnestness, what eagerness to clear yourselves, what indignation, what alarm, what longing, what concern, what readiness to see justice done. NIV

Godly sorrow is sanctifying, meaning it is a saving sorrow (v10 above), it causes a change in our hearts for the better, they become purer because we finally deal with the things in our lives that need to be dealt with. Laughter cannot do this, even though laughter is fine and acceptable, it does not help us to grow in a spiritual sense.

In recovery, it is not possible to progress unless godly sorrow is present. Worldly sorrow, the kind we have when we get caught acting out, is of no use. The sorrow talked about in our focus verse is godly sorrow; the kind that leads to repentance and change.

The Exercise – Write a description of how you initially felt when you "got caught" or maybe when you received a consequence for your "acting out" such as being fired, getting your sin exposed or losing a relationship. Almost none of us goes from acting out to godly sorrow without experiencing worldly sorrow, so this is likely to be a one or two paragraph picture of you experiencing the miserableness of feeling sorry for yourself.

Next write out a paragraph or two illustrating how you felt when you were overcome with godly sorrow. Describe what was happening in your life, what your feelings were and what new choices you were making. Did your purpose for being in recovery change? Were you doing recovery at first to save your marriage or comply with another person's demands or because your employer said so? Then, did it all change?

Help you sponsor or counselor understand how and why you moved from worldly to godly sorrow by being as thorough in this exercise as you can.

Sponsor Notes: _____

_____

_____

Useful Feeling Words:

- Sorry, Depressed, Worthless, Glad, Uplifted

Useful Attitudinal Words:

- Disbelief, Ignorant, Repentance, Incredulous, Relentlessness

My Pre-exercise Notes: _____

_____

_____

_____

_____

The suggested step for Exercise 26 is Step 7.

Exercise 27

Psalm 51:10-13

<u>Turning to God</u>

Ps 51:10-13 - Create in me a clean heart, O God, and renew a right spirit within me. Cast me not away from your presence, and take not your Holy Spirit from me. Restore to me the joy of your salvation, and uphold me with a willing spirit. Then I will teach transgressors your ways, and sinners will return to you. ESV

<u>Guiding Commentary</u> – Psalm 51 ranks as one of the most significant recovery oriented chapters in scripture. Psalm 51 is the prayer David penned out of his repentant heart, under the direction of the Holy Spirit. He did this after he had been confronted by Nathan the prophet about his adultery, stealing another man's wife and killing her husband. In this passage we see the author, David, pleading with God to stay with him and not cast him away. We see him also ask for God to clean his heart, and bring strength back to him. Lastly we see David make a promise to use this experience to teach the ways of God to other sinners for the purpose of evangelism.

It might also be helpful to read the story (2 Sam 12:1-15) of the confrontation of David by Nathan, remembering that David was the king, and could have anyone killed who opposed him. Nathan, courageously obeying God, confronts David in a very smooth way, and David is trapped by his own outrage. The story and the Psalm give us a picture of a godly confrontation and a godly response.

<u>The Exercise</u> – Discuss, in depth and in detail, times when you have prayed a similar prayer to the one in this passage. Use these questions to guide your answer. Have you pleaded with God to clean your heart, and bring you renewal? Have you asked Him to restore you in some way? Have you bargained with Him, telling Him you will do things for Him if He will just help you?

For those working through a Christian 12 Step program, are you going to incorporate David's promise at the end of this passage as part of your 12th step? If you are, explain in writing what you plan to do, if you are not, write out what you are going to do in your 12th step.

Sponsor Notes: _____

_____

_____

Useful Feeling Words:

- Outraged, Depressed, Shocked, Repentant, Dirty

Useful Attitudinal Words:

- Denial, Disbelief, Remorsefulness, Contriteness, Vulnerability

My Pre-exercise Notes: _____

_____

_____

_____

_____

The suggested step for Exercise 27 is Step 12.

Exercise 28

Psalm 51:6

Taking Personal Responsibility

Ps 51:6 - Behold, you delight in truth in the inward being, and you teach me wisdom in the secret heart. ESV

<u>Guiding Commentary</u> – This is from the great Psalm of David, written after he had been confronted with the truth about his affair with Bathsheba. In this verse we see that God, through David's words, is telling us what He wants from us; truth in our innermost being, sometimes called our heart or soul. God's response, shown in the second half of this verse, will be to bring us His wisdom in the area of life we are being truthful in.

It is a consistent theme in all of scripture that God wants us to take personal responsibility for our actions and their consequences. This is not for the purpose of condemning or judging us, it is so that we become open to the cleansing work He wants to do in us. It is always for our benefit, and the benefit of the people around us, and a great example of God's undying love for us.

<u>The Exercise</u> – Spend some time in reflection on why God desires truth in you, in your heart, in your "innermost being". Write out your <u>personal</u> answer to the question of why God desires this from YOU, use "I" and "me" statements in your answer. Don't focus on anybody else's faults or issues in your response (this avoids slipping into blaming others for your choices), as you write this do it with the understanding that it is between you and God.

After you have completed this, discuss times that you have changed some ungodly beliefs, values and attitudes to more godly ones. This is sometimes called exchanging a lie for the truth. Then talk about what God revealed to you as you moved to a more truthful life, and detail changes you have made in your behaviors as a result of being given more godly wisdom.

Sponsor Notes: _____

_____

_____

Useful Feeling Words:

- Glad, Expectant, Joyful, Excited, Cautious

Useful Attitudinal Words:

- Desirous, Stubbornness, Disbelieving, Negative, Positive

My Pre-exercise Notes: _____

_____

_____

_____

_____

The suggested step for Exercise 28 is Step 2.

Exercise 29

Psalms 103:3-5

<u>Hopelessness and Powerlessness</u>

Ps 103:3-5 - Who forgives all your iniquity, who heals all your diseases, who redeems your life from the pit, who crowns you with steadfast love and mercy, who satisfies you with good so that your youth is renewed like the eagle's. ESV

<u>Guiding Commentary</u> – God is challenging all of us in this set of verses to consider something. The core challenge is to ask us if we are our own god or is He God? He phrases it so that we must confess Him as God because we rationally understand that we cannot redeem our lives from the pit, we cannot forgive ourselves and we cannot bestow grace (lovingkindness) or compassion on ourselves. If we understand what is written in this scripture, we can see that we are actually helpless and powerless within ourselves to overcome our compulsions, our addictions and our sins.

<u>The Exercise</u> – Can you admit that you are, or have been, hopeless without God, that you are or were powerless over some things that control or controlled you? Write out, in detail, what you are or were powerless over. Show how this behavior or addiction took over your life; discuss the depths you would go to in hiding the problem, and how you chose a path of lying, cheating and stealing to feed the monster of your compulsions. Do your best to demonstrate in words how you were or are controlled.

Describe how you felt when you were "acting out", and then how you felt afterwards. How long was it before you reached the point where you "knew" that <u>you</u> were hopeless? Talk about the ups and downs of your sense of self-esteem?

If you have come through this and finally turned to God, talk about that experience, including expressions of emotions that you had during the process of moving from hopelessness to hopefulness.

Sponsor Notes: _____

_____

_____

Useful Feeling Words:

- Ashamed, Guilty, Impotent, Uncomfortable, Confused

Useful Attitudinal Words:

- Hopelessness, Powerlessness, Idolizing, Unsureness, Unworthiness

My Pre-exercise Notes: _____

_____

_____

_____

_____

The suggested step for Exercise 29 is Step 2.

Exercise 30

Psalms 121:1-2

<u>Finding Help</u>

Ps 121:1-2 - I lift up my eyes to the hills. From where does my help come? My help comes from the Lord, who made heaven and earth. ESV

<u>Guiding Commentary</u> – This is a statement of truth and recognition of real dependency on God. It recognizes that God is the creator, the source of life, and is the only one who truly knows us enough to help and heal us. In lifting our eyes up to Him, we are now no longer looking down. It is a moment when we admit we can't deal with our troubles ourselves and that we need Him. That is a healing moment in our lives, a moment when we start to allow the great physician to begin performing "soul surgery" on us. It can't be faked; it must done with a submission of heart.

<u>The Exercise</u> – Read the whole Psalm before moving to the exercise and be sure to take in the promises found in it. Particularly focus on verses 7 and 8, and claim these as yours in a short personal prayer as you start this work.

Have you ever submitted your heart to God, and looked to Him for help from your troubles? Or have you just looked to Him, expecting Him to help without doing anything on your part? All of us have most likely done some of each. In this exercise we are to confess some examples from our lives. In detail, write your story of the help you received detailing circumstances, what prayers or pleading you directed to God, how He answered (or didn't). Particularly note the people God put in your life who possibly were part of the way He helped you. Write a prayer of thanks to God for sending you those "helpers" and for others that have showed you grace during your time of restoration.

Sponsor Notes: _____

_____

_____

Useful Feeling Words:

- Powerless, Disbelief, Hopeless, Expectant, Thankful

Useful Attitudinal Words:

- Gratefulness, Incredulousness, Unbelieving, Questioning, Prideful

My Pre-exercise Notes: _____

_____

_____

_____

_____

The suggested step for Exercise 30 is Step 7.

Exercise 31

Proverbs 3:7-8

Refresh the Body

Prov 3:7-8 - Be not wise in your own eyes; fear the Lord, and turn away from evil. It will be healing to your flesh and refreshment to your bones. ESV

Guiding Commentary – One of the things that hinders successful recovery and the physical benefit of it is highlighted here. We all believe that we are wise. Some of us give superficial lip service to the idea that we have not "got it all together". We speak in our conversations about needing God's wisdom, and then we act like what He says is irrelevant or even wrong. When we "act out" in some way we are showing that we believe we are wiser than God. Is it any surprise that our spiritual health and often our physical health deteriorate? How many illnesses have we seen in ourselves and others that have their roots in internal distress, most often called stress? One of the causes of internal distress is the conflicts that go on inside us as we knowingly exercise our own wisdom against God's wisdom. God says here, don't do that! We are to not be wise in our own eyes; we are to fear Him, in the context of this exercise, meaning to respect Him and His vastly superior wisdom and we are to turn from evil. Then our bodies will receive healing and become refreshed and rested.

The Exercise – Think back to a time before recovery, a time when you thought you had things together. Discuss some of the choices you made in your own wisdom, and if you can, speak to if you made these choices knowing they contradicted God's word. Be specific, for example, I knew I shouldn't have gone into that massage parlor, but I was looking for some action, or I knew that I shouldn't have gone to bed with this guy, but he was so hot. As you construct a word picture of some of your unwise choices, connect them to some of the emotions you felt once you realized what you had done. Also answer the question of how they affected you physically. Did your health start to deteriorate? Were there new allergies, illnesses or did you get physically run down and maybe couldn't sleep well?

Now move forward to the present day. Are you beginning to make more godly choices? Talk about them and compare them to choices you used to make. Then also discuss if they have resulted in better psychological health, meaning less negative emotions like guilt and shame. Then discuss if you are getting more rest, if your medical condition is improving and you are less "stressed out".

Do you think you are learning to "fear God" more? Discuss how that feels for you. When you "fear God" are you actually afraid, or are you sensing something different?

Tell your sponsor or mentor, as you write out your exercise answer, how you plan to implement making more godly choices in the future, and do this using concrete and specific examples.

Sponsor Notes: _____

_____

_____

Useful Feeling Words:

- Fearful, Hurt, Shame, Guilty, Convicted

Useful Attitudinal Words:

- Rebelliousness, Prideful, Disbelief, Denial, Seeking

My Pre-exercise Notes: _____

_____

_____

_____

_____

The suggested step for Exercise 31 is Step 4.

Exercise 32

Proverbs 18:21

The Power of the Tongue

Prov 18:21 - Death and life are in the power of the tongue, and those who love it will eat its fruits. ESV

Guiding Commentary – This is one of the many scriptures that deal with the subject of how we use our tongue. In this proverb God speaks to us about how powerful the tongue really is. He says the tongue has death and life in it, and that how we use our own tongue will determine our life's circumstances. For some this can mean if we choose to verbally reject God we will have spiritual death and be headed to Hell. Or, we can verbally choose Christ and be spiritually reborn, or made eternally alive. And yet there are other meanings. One of the most important is that of building and sustaining healthy relationships by the things we say as a fruit giving life, or destroying relationships through the things we say as a fruit giving death. In recovery we also recognize that when we were acting out we would lie extensively, meaning, in the context of our verse, that we would use our tongue sinfully and it would lead us toward a living death of being in our compulsions or addictions.

The Exercise – Can you identify with the message of this scripture? In this exercise we are going to explore how we have used our tongue to build up or destroy relationships. First go back as far as you reasonably can and look at how you used the tongue in conducting your life. Explore how you used it to lie, manipulate, or coerce other people into giving you what you wanted. Do this by naming the individuals concerned, identifying the way you used your tongue, then talk about the health of the relationship, if it still exists, and finally declare this relationship alive or dead, or somewhere in between. If one of these relationships has been recovered and is now healthy, talk about how that happened.

Now explore your behavior, in the context of how you are using your tongue in relationships, since you entered recovery. Are you lying less? Is speaking the truth still a struggle? Talk about how your relationships have improved in quality since you changed how you behave with your tongue. Name some significant relationships, such as spousal, parental or children, coworkers and church friends and talk about how these relationships have improved as you have used your tongue in new life-giving ways.

Add any other observations about how your life has changed since you began to use your tongue to speak more truth than when you were in your compulsions or addictions.

Sponsor Notes: _____

_____

_____

Useful Feeling Words:

- Guilt, Pride, Afraid, Conflicted, Confused

Useful Attitudinal Words:

- Condemning, Judgmental, Boasting, Shaming, Resentment

My Pre-exercise Notes: _____

_____

_____

_____

_____

The suggested step for Exercise 32 is Step 5.

Exercise 33

Psalms 31:7-8

<u>Praying for Deliverance</u>

Ps 31:7-8 - I will rejoice and be glad in your steadfast love, because you have seen my affliction; you have known the distress of my soul, and you have not delivered me into the hand of the enemy; you have set my feet in a broad place. ESV

<u>Guiding Commentary</u> – The first eight verses of Psalm 31 are a plea for deliverance from trouble combined with an acknowledgement of who God is and that He can help us.

In our focus verses we see that as we pray for deliverance or rescue from the trouble we are in we must agree with God that because we have already begun to sense His healing, we know that He knows how we feel. Our Psalmist calls this "anguish of my soul" and all of us in recovery have felt it.

Then in verse 8 we see the writer recognize another truth, that God has not simply let him go and become a victim of *an* "enemy" or worse than that *the* enemy. The Psalmist also says that God has put our feet on solid ground, which is Him and His word, and if we are correctly positioned, within His church.

Particularly in the early stages of recovery this realization that God can rescue us, that He has the power, the knowhow, the resources and the willingness to help us is important. In fact we probably ought to not move into the detailed confessional stage (Step 4 and beyond in the 12 steps) of our recovery until we come to grips with this. No matter where we are in our recovery it is wise to revisit the thoughts expressed in this Psalm; it helps us to retain perspective.

<u>The Exercise</u> – Write out a prayer for your personal deliverance from the enemies you face. Try to write this prayer from a submissive attitude, recognizing that God is supreme and you are fallen, and that He has the power, knowhow, resources and willingness to help you. To help with this we are suggesting the following format:

1. A paragraph of acknowledgement of who and what God is to you.

2. A paragraph confessing and stating your troubles as best you know them.
3. A paragraph identifying the enemies and barriers you have to healing.
4. A paragraph stating that you know and understand that God feels what you feel.
5. A paragraph expressing confidence in God's ability to get you through this.
6. A paragraph of thanks for the ingredients of recovery He has placed in your life.
7. A paragraph containing your personal promise to God that you will do your part.

Sponsor Notes: _____

_____

_____

Useful Feeling Words:

- Afraid, Cautious, Willing, Pained, Troubled

Useful Attitudinal Words:

- Fearful, Punishment, Shaming, Expectant, Willing

My Pre-exercise Notes: _____

_____

_____

_____

_____

The suggested step for Exercise 33 is Step 3.

Exercise 34

Psalms 6:1-4

<u>Waiting on God</u>

Ps 6:1-4 - O Lord, rebuke me not in your anger, nor discipline me in your wrath. Be gracious to me, O Lord, for I am languishing; heal me, O Lord, for my bones are troubled. My soul also is greatly troubled. But you, O Lord - how long? Turn, O Lord, deliver my life; save me for the sake of your steadfast love. ESV

<u>Guiding Commentary</u> – In this Psalm we see a prayer to God that most of us in recovery probably have said in our own words at some time, particularly in the early months of our recovery journey. Look at the component parts. In the first part we see a person who recognizes that their sin has put them in a position where God has a right to be angry, and deal with them in His holy wrath. He asks for God's merciful grace in the throes of his depression. He says his "bones are dismayed" and also that his "soul is dismayed", meaning that he is experiencing the consequences of his actions in his body and in his inner person. And we see here that the author is asking that question we all seem to ask, "How long is it before you heal me God"? The author, thought to be King David, then pleads with God, please rescue me, and please save me from the consequences of all that I have done because you are a loving and kind God.

<u>The Exercise</u> – Write about your early experiences in recovery in the context of this passage. Give a description of the time when you finally reached the understanding that you needed to change direction, which we call repentance. Then talk about how this sense of knowing that God is completely justified in being angry with your behavior, bringing you to whatever punishment He determines is necessary, finally hit home with you. Were you "dismayed in your bones and soul"? Did you slip into depression or physical illness? Did you pray a prayer similar to the one above; did impatience with God and His timing grab you as you fought to regain some form of normalcy in your life again? Did you finally throw yourself on His mercy, abandoning your own attempts to fix your problems, and plead for Him to come and rescue you from the pit you were in?

Write this story about your despair, your fears that this time of trouble would never end; your time of depression and grief; your pleading with God to rescue you, and how He answered you. End it with a written prayer of thanksgiving for how He came through for you when the time was right.

Sponsor Notes: _____

_____

_____

Useful Feeling Words:

- Impatient, Nervous, Wanting, Ready, Bored

Useful Attitudinal Words:

- Impatience, Afraid, Expectant, Resentment, Taking

My Pre-exercise Notes: _____

_____

_____

_____

_____

The suggested step for Exercise 34 is Step 7.

Exercise 35

Proverbs 11:20

<u>Becoming a Delight to God</u>

*Prov 11:20 - Those of crooked heart are an abomination to the Lord, but those of blameless ways are his delight. **ESV***

<u>Guiding Commentary</u> – In this scripture we see the typical contrasts found throughout the book of Proverbs. This example is comparing a perverse heart with a blameless one. A perverse heart is a heart that is occupied by ungodly values, beliefs and attitudes. These are heart characteristics that stand against God in our lives and He says in our scripture that a person with such a heart is an "abomination" to Him. When we were acting out, we were demonstrating to all who could see it, the ungodly values, beliefs and attitudes located in our heart; this means that we were an abomination to Him. This truth is sometimes hard to swallow about ourselves, especially if our behaviors are "not that bad" like people-pleasing (codependency) or workaholism. The problem is that when we focus on the behavior we miss the perverseness of our hearts. How do we deal with this? God says here that we are to work on becoming "blameless". In this context it means to replace ungodly values, beliefs and attitudes with His values, beliefs and attitudes. That is how we will become blameless.

<u>The Exercise</u> – In recovery there is an expression that is used to describe our growth or change that applies here. It is, "Progress not Perfection". It is an impossibility for us to change a perverse heart to a blameless one quickly and easily; that means we have to work on it each day. In doing this we move slowly from perverseness to blamelessness. In this exercise we want to look at what our values, beliefs and attitudes were before we entered recovery and compare them to what they are now.

Start by identifying an acting out behavior and then identify what values, beliefs and attitudes that behavior seems to indicate that you used to have. For example, if you smoked weed as an adolescent, were you rebellious in attitude, did you believe that this would solve the emotional state you were in, and did you value smoking this over going to God to deal with problems? Do this for all the significant acting out behaviors you can identify from your past. When you've finished, look at the exercise and determine if there is a pattern.

Next, identify your current and new (since entering recovery) behaviors, and ascertain the new values, beliefs and attitudes you are displaying. Finally try to determine if these heart characteristics are godly or not. If you know some scripture references that can confirm this to you, record them.

Lastly, how do you feel about the "progress" you have made?

Sponsor Notes: _____

_____

_____

Useful Feeling Words:

- Thankful, Glad, Exalted, Prideful, Guilty

Useful Attitudinal Words:

- Blamelessness, Perverseness, Desiring, Pride, Arrogance

My Pre-exercise Notes: _____

_____

_____

_____

_____

The suggested step for Exercise 35 is Step 11.

Exercise 36

Ecclesiastes 8:5-6

<u>Time for Amends?</u>

Eccl 8:5-6 - Whoever keeps a command will know no evil thing, and the wise heart will know the proper time and the just way. For there is a time and a way for everything, although man's trouble lies heavy on him. ESV

<u>Guiding Commentary</u> – One of the important aspects of recovery that is sometimes rushed through or minimized is that of amends, or using an old word, restitution. Elsewhere in scripture, particularly in the books of the law, this is established as a principle of how to live. In this scripture we see God reminding us, in the context of amends, that there is a proper time and procedure to the making of amends, even if the need for amends is weighing on us.

Speaking of being honestly sorry to someone and making it right starts with an attitude, an attitude of willingness. That is the first part of the "procedure" that this scripture talks about. The second part is making a list of those we have harmed. If we have a sponsor or mentor, their help with this second part is almost invaluable. Then as we look at each person on the list, our sponsor will help us identify the people we "have to" make amends to, and those we ought to not contact. Examples of the people we ought to not contact are old sexual acting out partners, as they may have moved on and are married, or individuals we have abused. In both of these cases, we actually do more harm than good.

The Twelve Steps say this well when it talks about being willing to make amends but not doing harm to anyone as a result. It captures the essence of God's position that we ought to be totally willing to "make it right."

This scripture uses the word "misery" and that definitely describes how we feel going through this "amends" procedure. And we will discover how freeing it is when we finally make amends and the misery lifts; because God honors and blesses those obey Him in this matter.

<u>The Exercise</u> – Do you struggle and mentally sweat profusely when you think about having to face those you may have hurt or harmed in some way? Write

about how you feel about this process or procedure of amends. In your expression of what you think and feel about this address your sense of the spiritual shape of your heart in the context of your attitude of willingness to make amends. Write how you are or are not looking forward to this. Does something about amends make you nervous, are you feeling miserable, or are you excited to finally make things right? Are you struggling because you are "pain avoidant"? If so write a short paragraph on how this connects to pain avoidance earlier in your life.

Sponsor Notes: _____

_____

_____

Useful Feeling Words:

- Afraid, Apprehensive, Avoidant, Miserable, Depressed

Useful Attitudinal Words:

- Fearful, Resentment, Anxious, Pessimistic, Somber

My Pre-exercise Notes: _____

_____

_____

_____

_____

The suggested step for Exercise 36 is Step 8.

Exercise 37

Psalms 97:9

Turn to the Supreme One

Ps 97:9 - For you, O Lord, are most high over all the earth; you are exalted far above all gods. ESV

Guiding Commentary – In this simple statement the Psalmist under the guidance of the Holy Spirit speaks possibly the greatest truth that exists. The One True God is above all other gods. Other versions of this verse use the word "supreme."

In Christian recovery this is a fundamental belief, a foundation upon which all of our work is built. We must believe that He is supreme over all the other gods that exist. These other gods in our lives might be pleasures, people, power, or even some of the old standbys of sex, drugs and rock 'n roll. God almighty is above all these things, He existed before they did, He created the world in which they function and He is the only one who knows how to overcome them. Seeking help from Him leads to healing, while seeking help from the world at best will lead to relief which is the highest level of failure available without the "Supreme One."

In Christian recovery it is Christ that saves, He saves us from our other gods that do not seek the best for us, because they suck us dry in every way. All of us face this choice; am I going to allow Christ to lead me through this, through His word (Bible), His Holy Spirit and His people (Christ-centered recovery group) or am I going to choose to go my own way?

And, just in case a person reading this has never heard this, Jesus Christ is God, the same God who made everything, and He chose to come to the earth He made to show us the way in all things.

The Exercise – This exercise is a time to declare what you believe about God. Write out an extensive statement of what you believe about God. State whether you believe He exists, whether He is supreme in your view and can help you. State whether you believe Jesus is God, and will save you from the other gods or idols in your life. State whether you are willing to let Him have rule and reign over your life. State whether you are willing to submit to His direction, even if it means

76

taking instruction through other imperfect people, those further down the road in Christian recovery.

Lay it all out, and go all in!

Sponsor Notes: _____

_____

_____

Useful Feeling Words:

- Angry, Oppressed, Frustrated, Sad, Stressed

Useful Attitudinal Words:

- Gladness, Punishment, Judgment, Victimhood, Gratefulness

My Pre-exercise Notes: _____

_____

_____

_____

The suggested step for Exercise 37 is Step 2.

Exercise 38

Psalm 32:3-5

Daily Confession

Ps 32:3-5 - For when I kept silent, my bones wasted away through my groaning all day long. For day and night your hand was heavy upon me; my strength was dried up as by the heat of summer. I acknowledged my sin to you, and I did not cover my iniquity; I said, "I will confess my transgressions to the Lord," and you forgave the iniquity of my sin. ESV

Guiding Commentary – In this part of Psalm 32 we see David, the human author, speak about some important recovery principles. In the selected section we see that we are told that when we keep silent our bones "waste away" which is an ancient description of feeling down, or depressed. In our context today this means that as we don't speak about the things that we need to get out of our inner person, the knowledge of our sins, the impure thoughts, and the withholding of our agreement with God (confession) then we are going to become emotionally down. Then David moves to a truth that when we don't do this (speak about our stuff), the Lord will put His "heavy hand" on us, which is a term for His discipline (see Heb 12:4-12), and that His discipline will sap our strength. This discipline is designed to progressively encourage us to go to God with whatever we ought to. (As an FYI, this not only applies to confession, but also applies when God wants to communicate with us about other matters) Finally David says that after he confessed his issues, and quit covering them up, he was relieved of his guilt burden through God's forgiveness (1 Jn 1:9).

The Exercise – Be sure to also read Heb 12:4-12 before you start this exercise.

Have you noticed that when you don't deal with things that come up in your life that they seem to weigh on you? Write about two or maybe three of these times in your life that have occurred since you began recovery. Detail out the situation and any other relevant background and describe how you felt, using at least 3 feeling words. Talk about how "down" you felt, and if you sensed God's "heavy hand of discipline" weighing on you, as well as the guilt that you may having been holding on to. Did you eventually come to realize that you needed to deal with it? Talk about how you got to that point, for example you went back to your counselor, or maybe you confessed the issue to your spouse, your sponsor or God.

Finally, did these events lead you to becoming more diligent in the spiritual discipline of daily confession? If not, why not? If you are practicing daily confession, have you found it helpful in the elimination of unwanted emotional down times in your life? What would you advise others about this subject?

Sponsor Notes: _____

_____

_____

Useful Feeling Words:

- Wasting away, Depressed, Angry, Relieved, Numb

Useful Attitudinal Words:

- Disillusionment, Loneliness, Gladness, Isolating, Resentment

My Pre-exercise Notes: _____

_____

_____

_____

_____

The suggested step for Exercise 38 is Step 10.

Exercise 39

Ecclesiastes 11:4

Recovery Doesn't Just Happen

Eccl 11:4 - He who observes the wind will not sow, and he who regards the clouds will not reap. ESV

Guiding Commentary – There is a general principle in life called reaping and sowing, and it is found throughout scripture. Some of the places to cross check our verse here with are 2 Cor 9:6, 2 Thess 3:6-13 and particularly Gal 6:7-9. In our selected verse we see a focus on the people who wait to sow; it says these individuals will not reap.

One of the biggest mistakes those in recovery can make is to "wait for the right time" to begin working. This is notably true for those who procrastinate about getting their moral inventory done. We see and hear the excuses. It reminds us of the old "the dog ate my homework" excuse given by kids in high school. Some common excuses we have heard for not getting on with recovery work are; I'm busy at work, my wife needs me to do something, the kids have got me on a hectic schedule and the granddaddy of them all, I'm waiting for God to prompt me.

This may be tough to hear, but it is so simple to get; **there is no valid excuse for not getting on with recovery work**. This doesn't mean that one can't take short breaks, but these are small rest periods, and we must go right back to work.

Christian recovery can be thought of as weeding out the bad and sowing the good so that we can receive a harvest of a better life. When we "get on with it" every person in our lives will benefit from it; ourselves, our spouses, our kids, our co-workers, our neighbors and most importantly our God.

The Exercise – Have you put off "getting on with it?" Write about your reluctance to work on your recovery. (We have all been there.) Try to identify the excuses, which we often call reasons, which you have used with yourself and others that you put up as barriers to "getting on with it." Do you agree with what is says above about there being no excuses for not getting on with your work?

As you do this exercise, include a couple of sentences about the feelings that come up for you. This could include feelings of guilt, shame, disappointment, depression or even resentment at having to address this. These will be good points for your sponsor or counselor to focus on during the time you go over your response to this scripture.

Sponsor Notes: _____

_____

_____

Useful Feeling Words:

- Fearful, Avoidant, Burdened, Scared, Withdrawing

Useful Attitudinal Words:

- Powerlessness, Victimhood, Fearfulness, Anxious, Agitated

My Pre-exercise Notes: _____

_____

_____

_____

_____

The suggested step for Exercise 39 is Step 4.

Exercise 40

Proverbs 20:9

<u>Ongoing Cleansing</u>

Prov 20:9 - Who can say, "I have made my heart pure; I am clean from my sin"? ESV

<u>Guiding Commentary</u> – This simple verse highlights a common problem for those in recovery. We do the work, we make amends, and our lives get immeasurably better, then we stop working because inside us we believe the lie that we are "fixed." What might be true is that we have come a long, long way and are living openly and honestly, and are doing our best to live in godly ways. The problem is that there is almost always more things to deal with, and these things only get revealed by God through His Holy Spirit. There may be deep hurts that need to be uncovered, or hidden attitudes that begin to spring up inside us. There is always the specter of relapse as well! In true recovery we must say that we are never finished working, and echoing the sentiment of the verse, we should not take the attitude that we "have it all together." Recovery must become a lifestyle choice, with ongoing cleansing.

<u>The Exercise</u> – For those new (a year or less) to recovery, you may have experienced some relief from the burdens that come with acting out. Are you tempted to "take your foot off the gas pedal?" Write about the relief that has come into your life, and answer the question, "Have I backed off from working my recovery program?" Try to identify temptations or distractions, and their sources, which are stopping you from working.

For those with significant experience in recovery, have you backed off in your efforts to work your program? If you have, write out your description of this, talk about how you have let go of some recovery principles, and what has moved your focus from taking appropriate care of yourself to doing something different. If you are strong in your personal recovery program, tell us how you maintained yourself in this. Write out how you were tempted to drop recovery, or back off, and how distractions may have come into your life, and what you did as a response.

Sponsor Notes: _____

_____

_____

Useful Feeling Words:

- Dishonest, Stressed, Surrendered, Anxiety, Fearful

Useful Attitudinal Words:

- Thankfulness, Anxious, Fearfulness, Rebelliousness, Disobedient

My Pre-exercise Notes: _____

_____

_____

_____

_____

The suggested step for Exercise 40 is Step 10.

Exercise 41

Psalms 40:11-12

Compassion for Defects

Ps 40:11-12 - As for you, O Lord, you will not restrain your mercy from me; your steadfast love and your faithfulness will ever preserve me! For evils have encompassed me beyond number; my iniquities have overtaken me, and I cannot see; they are more than the hairs of my head; my heart fails me. ESV

Guiding Commentary – In Psalm 40 we see a confession of deliverance, an acknowledgement that it is God, and God alone, who can lift us out of the pit we are in. This has several applications to Christian recovery. The application we are looking at here is one where we know that there are several things inside of us that have led to our poor decisions, and we need to remove these defects, whatever they are, from our souls.

By the time we've been in recovery for a while we have learned that our troubles, caused through our character defects, are not a simple thing to explain. In looking at them we have discovered that they are many (a multitude is how the Psalmist puts it), that they have overwhelmed us and that we cannot see them in our own power. We might even agree with the Psalm by saying they are numerous and just thinking about it causes us to feel overcome.

God is helping us here to understand that our emphasis in dealing with our many defects ought to be on requesting His compassion and His truth in cleaning up our act.

The Exercise – At some point we are all going to ask God to help us. In this exercise, we want to write out a prayer to God confessing all the character defects we know of, and asking Him to be compassionate with us by helping us see them clearly and removing them from within us. Be sure to not minimize the bigness of these defects as some of us in recovery tend to do. You may even compare your defects to His incorruptible perfection to achieve appropriate perspective.

As you write this prayer, acknowledge your own personal powerlessness to change yourself, and as best as you can, remembering there is no perfect way, throw yourself verbally at God's feet.

After you write this prayer, spend the next 7 days praying it over yourself. When you have done this, write in your journal about the experience. After writing, discuss with your godly advisors.

Sponsor Notes: _____

_____

_____

Useful Feeling Words:

- Impotent, Weak, Confused, Ashamed, Exposed

Useful Attitudinal Words:

- Anxious, Fearfulness, Weakness, Insecurity, Resentment

My Pre-exercise Notes: _____

_____

_____

_____

_____

The suggested step for Exercise 41 is Step 7.

Exercise 42

Proverbs 3:1-2

Living the Life

Prov 3:1-2 - My son, do not forget my teaching, but let your heart keep my commandments, for length of days and years of life and peace they will add to you. **ESV**

Guiding Commentary – This is a simple piece of wisdom literature to anyone who has allowed themselves time to be taught by God, usually through study, listening to others such as preachers, teachers and through prayer and meditation. Scriptures, inspired by the Holy Spirit (2 Tim 3:16-17), and the Holy Spirit himself are the only source of truth. Here, God is promising that as we remember His truth, lodge it in our hearts, and practice His commands and instructions our lives will be prolonged and will have prosperity.

A word of caution here! This passage has often been misused by some who preach and teach it to mean that if we obey God we will have whatever we want; notably excellent or renewed health resulting in long life or high material wealth. This is bad understanding and is theological error. What it actually means is that our lives would be longer and our prosperity (spiritual, psychological, physical and material, for example) would be greater than if we don't follow and obey God.

In Christian recovery this is a fundamental principle (also true for secular recovery, even if they are unbelievers). We hear and learn how to conduct our lives in a new way, a way that honors God. Once we have done the work of confession, repentance and placing our hearts in God's care, we have learned to live all of our lives as if we are in recovery every moment. For some of us our lives may have been saved, for some of us we have come back to sanity. However recovery has affected us, we have become more prosperous in ways we never thought possible. We learn to practice recovery each and every day because it is life saving!

The Exercise – In this exercise we want to focus on the need to "live the life" by living by the principles of Christian recovery. The written part of this exercise is to write one or two sentences or a small paragraph, in the manner of an encyclopedia, about up to 10 guiding principles of Christian recovery. We'll give you one here as an example (which you can use if you choose):

- <u>God is always right</u>. When I believe or think or act in ways that are contrary to scripture, it is I that am wrong. This means I have to work on correcting my thinking, my beliefs and my behaviors.

After you have completed this exercise to your satisfaction, discuss it with your sponsor, counselor or mentor. (Note also that this list can be used by a person to run their life.)

Sponsor Notes: _____

_____

_____

Useful Feeling Words:

- Overwhelmed, Excited, Grateful, Joyful, Relieved

Useful Attitudinal Words:

- Thankfulness, Resentment, Annoyed, Avoidance, Appreciative

My Pre-exercise Notes: _____

_____

_____

_____

_____

The suggested step for Exercise 42 is Step 10.

Exercise 43

Proverbs 6:16-19

<u>Abominations to Avoid</u>

Prov 6:16-19 - There are six things that the Lord hates, seven that are an abomination to him: haughty eyes, a lying tongue, and hands that shed innocent blood, a heart that devises wicked plans, feet that make haste to run to evil, a false witness who breathes out lies, and one who sows discord among brothers. ESV

<u>Guiding Commentary</u> – This little section of scripture provides a graphic reminder of what God opposes with great passion. An abomination is a morally disgusting thing. Let's see what these seven abominations are; pride, lying, murder, a wicked heart, a person that proactively seeks evil things to do, a liar and an antagonist. When we look at this list from the perspective of a person in recovery we can identify with most if not all of these. While we were still acting out, we were prideful, we constantly lied, we got angry with others (Mt 5:22), we schemed to get our compulsive desires met, we gleefully sought out our evil pleasures, we were proficient liars and we caused strife in the lives of those around us. Before recovery we were the poster children for abomination, but after we began to accept God's discipline we moved out of a life of dark abomination and into a life characterized by truth and grace.

<u>The Exercise</u> – Take each of these seven abominations separately and identify a time, a situation or an event that demonstrates that you were acting out in some way and which abomination was at work in you. Restrict yourself to one description for each of the seven abominations. Some of us may have trouble identifying with the abomination of murder, in this case use the definition of murder used by Jesus in Mt 7:22, that of intense anger toward a person.

Assuming that you have been working diligently in recovery, you would have made progress in all of these abominations. First grade yourself on your progress, then prioritize which of the seven still needs the most work first and list them down to the last. Finally, celebrate with a friend or two the progress you have already made in removing abominations from your life by doing something you like to do that is not an abomination!

Sponsor Notes: _____

_____

_____

Useful Feeling Words:

- Remorse, Sorry, Guilty, Angry, Disillusioned, Upset

Useful Attitudinal Words:

- Gratefulness, Sorrowfulness, Disturbed, Remorseful, Sadness

My Pre-exercise Notes: _____

_____

_____

_____

_____

The suggested step for Exercise 43 is Step 5.

Exercise 44

Ecclesiastes 4:9-12

<u>Loners Fall</u>

Eccl 4:9-12 - Two are better than one, because they have a good reward for their toil. For if they fall, one will lift up his fellow. But woe to him who is alone when he falls and has not another to lift him up! Again, if two lie together, they keep warm, but how can one keep warm alone? And though a man might prevail against one who is alone, two will withstand him—a threefold cord is not quickly broken. ESV

<u>Guiding Commentary</u> – Like a lot of the wisdom in Ecclesiastes this is spoken by God through the human author in plain language. In recovery we know the principle stated here is a fundamental reality for our success in getting through, overcoming and healing from our troubles. Without others we simply will not be able to do it. Just as surely as we need God's direction and help we need His people's direction and help.

In these verses we see that the efforts of two working together have a greater success than the efforts of two individuals added together. This is why we have sponsors, counselors and other godly advisors. We see that if one of us falls, meaning slips or relapses, then others can help him or her, but this is obviously not true for the individual who tries recovery alone. The next big point from this verse is that when we are attacked, and we will be, our greatest protection is the people that God has arranged in our life to stand with us in the recovery battle. Finally, in all of these points, two is good, but three is better, meaning that having one person walk with us is good, but having two is better. We have found that it is hard to have too many, but having at least four close advisors seems to work for most people.

<u>The Exercise</u> – Think about your life in recovery so far. Have you experienced yourself, or witnessed in others, the principle of not going it alone in recovery? Do you believe the guidance found above is true? Write out a couple of short paragraphs describing situations where you or others have tried to go it alone and struggled, but don't identify people other than yourself by name to respect others confidentiality.

Separately, list the names of up to four people that know your story and that you would turn to for help when your struggles come up for you. Write out a prayer about each of them. Include thanks to God for putting them in your life, include a petition to God to keep them safe and sound, include a prayer for their spiritual health and finally include a prayer for their protection from the unseen enemies around us. Of course, add anything else God puts on your heart to pray for about them. Pray by reading out loud each of these prayers each day for one week.

Sponsor Notes: _____

_____

_____

Useful Feeling Words:

- Glad, Grateful, Joyful, Encouraged, Confident

Useful Attitudinal Words:

- Gladness, Jubilant, Expectant, Appreciative, Joyfulness

My Pre-exercise Notes: _____

_____

_____

_____

The suggested step for Exercise 44 is Step 12.

Exercise 45

Proverbs 25:8

Be Careful With Amends

Prov 25:8 - Do not hastily bring into court, for what will you do in the end, when your neighbor puts you to shame? ESV

Guiding Commentary – In this strange sounding proverb we see a well crafted warning for those of us in recovery. When we get ready to make amends, admit our faults and ask for forgiveness, or pay restitution there is one thing that all experienced recovery guides will address, and it is probably the wisest thing of all to do in this necessary action. That is to do it slowly and with great care in doing our best to determine the consequences before we act.

This verse speaks of the futility of making amends if we end up being in a worse state than before we did; it says our neighbor, the person we make amends to, may put us to shame. In scriptural parlance shame was used to describe emotional states of personal desolation, worthlessness, powerlessness and hopelessness, much like we may have felt going into recovery.

Making amends can be harmful to us and the other person, and piling on harm to previous injury is not smart, whether it is others or ourselves. We must find alternative methods of making amends than direct one-on-one or face-to-face encounters in some situations.

This does not absolve us of making amends or provide us with an easy way out, a way of avoiding this difficult action. In fact it makes it harder, because the true making of amends with godly sorrow is very healing and not making them is a serious issue for the integrity of our program. This is why making amends needs to be done under the guidance of an experienced and knowledgeable mentor.

The Exercise – In this exercise we are going to assume that you have a list of names and associated actions that you have taken that harmed them in the past.

Take the most important five (but you can do more if you wish) and spend time with each name, meditating on it and the possible effect amends will have on you, on your spouse and children (if you have them), on your employer and on any other significant person in your life. Do not do this lightly; give the Holy Spirit time to work in you to assist you in getting to a thorough answer. Write down everything that comes to you.

Then do the same thing for each name, but consider the other person, their spouse, children, employer etc.

Finally, get with your sponsor, counselor, mentor or other guide and sort all these things out to make some sense of them.

Sponsor Notes: _____

_____

_____

Useful Feeling Words:

- Cautious, Careful, Thankful, Wary, Fearful

Useful Attitudinal Words:

- Gratefulness, Carefulness, Anxiousness, Foreboding, Agitated

My Pre-exercise Notes: _____

_____

_____

_____

The suggested step for Exercise 45 is Step 9.

Exercise 46

Proverbs 30:7-9

<u>Recovery Has its Own Pace</u>

Prov 30:7-9 - Two things I ask of you; deny them not to me before I die: Remove far from me falsehood and lying; give me neither poverty nor riches; feed me with the food that is needful for me, lest I be full and deny you and say, "Who is the Lord?" or lest I be poor and steal and profane the name of my God. ESV

<u>Guiding Commentary</u> – This is a prayer hidden in a proverb. Our writer asks a simple enough request which we can all identify with; we are to paraphrase it for our use here.

- Lord, please give me enough to get by on, I am afraid of being tempted by having too much, because I may start to believe I did it myself, and not give You the credit. And I am also afraid of having too little that I may take matters into my own hands by stealing what You have given to others. Either side of this will dishonor you God, and I don't ever want to do that.

In Christian recovery we may face a similar dilemma of temptation. If God gives us relief and healing in abundance and we start to see significant progress in overcoming our compulsions and addictions, we may be tempted to think and then believe we have done it under our own power. If we are not feeling or sensing that we are making much progress, we may be tempted to feel like He is not with us and that we are poor in spirit; we may also be tempted to push our recovery along by spiritually stealing through lying about our real progress. We spiritually steal in our Christian recovery by hiding the truth and withholding how we are really feeling and what we are really thinking from our godly advisors.

<u>The Exercise</u> – Begin by taking a look at the complete picture of your Christian recovery so far. Remember the basic Christian recovery principle that if we ask God to be involved in our recovery, then He will dictate its pace. Start the written part of this exercise by writing out one example each, from your personal experiences in recovery, of where you felt like you "had it all together" and where you were "spiritually stealing" (as defined above).

The last written part of this exercise is to write a personal prayer of apology to God for how you may have dishonored Him through your recovery. Include a request for His forgiveness (1 Jn 1:9) and a request for Him to help you see the two temptations (pride and spiritual stealing), which both lead to the sin of dishonoring God, in the future.

Finally contact any of your godly advisors you may have misled in your recovery past, and make amends to them.

Sponsor Notes: _____

_____

_____

Useful Feeling Words:

- Tempted, Ashamed, Confused, Impatient, Wounded

Useful Attitudinal Words:

- Vulnerable, Reticent, Resentfulness, Thankfulness, Confident

My Pre-exercise Notes: _____

_____

_____

_____

_____

The suggested step for Exercise 46 is Step 7.

Exercise 47

Psalms 20:4-5

<u>Bless Someone</u>

Ps 20:4-5 - May he grant you your heart's desire and fulfill all your plans! May we shout for joy over your salvation, and in the name of our God set up our banners! May the Lord fulfill all your petitions! ESV

<u>Guiding Commentary</u> – This Psalm is a prayer about achieving victory over enemies. The verses shown here are verses of encouragement.

There are times in our recovery struggles when we feel overwhelmed, discouraged, beaten down, depressed, fatigued, or lonely. It is in these moments that we need our fellow strugglers to come alongside us to lift us up, encourage us and revive our flagging souls.

Equally important for us to acknowledge is that we sometimes feel that things are going well, we are stronger, recovery is working well and our struggles are not overwhelming us. These are times to enjoy, and they are also times to go to those who are behind us on the path of recovery to lift them up. When God has done a great work in us, we will be grateful and we will want to thank Him in some way. Is there a better way than to go and encourage others with messages like we see in our focus verses?

<u>The Exercise</u> – Memorize the scripture above in any version you choose, then find at least three people of the same gender within your recovery group that are behind you on the path of recovery. Go to each one separately and ask permission to pray these two verses over them. To avoid being rejected, explain to them that it is part of your own recovery to give back to others what you have been given. Talk with them afterward about what these scriptures mean to you.

After each session, write down or journal about your experience. Include in your journal these factors; what it was like, if you were afraid, how you felt afterward, both immediately and after some time, and if you would be comfortable doing it again if the Holy Spirit prompted you. Discuss these conclusions with your sponsor, counselor or mentor.

Sponsor Notes: _____

_____

_____

Useful Feeling Words:

- Grateful, Happy, Blessed, Honored, Ready

Useful Attitudinal Words:

- Thankfulness, Cheerfulness, Readiness, Servant-heartedness, Activated

My Pre-exercise Notes: _____

_____

_____

_____

_____

The suggested step for Exercise 47 is Step 12.

Exercise 48

Proverbs 20:9

<u>Prudent Avoidance</u>

Prov 22:3 - The prudent sees danger and hides himself, but the simple go on and suffer for it. ESV

<u>Guiding Commentary</u> – Prudence is the wise handling of practical matters, or can also be thought of as exercising good judgment or common sense. Scripturally, here in our verse and others it indicates caution as well as wisdom and good judgment.

Before recovery we were all less than prudent. We can say this because if we were prudent, we wouldn't have made all those unwise choices, or rushed into pleasing our senses without thinking. In this verse we see a call to prudence, to looking ahead into the area of possible consequences before we choose a course of action. We are instructed to hide ourselves from potential danger. An example here would be a problem drinker not going into a bar he or she used to frequent.

The verse contrasts being prudent with being simple. Usually we would say simple is a good thing, but scripture uses the word differently. The root of the Hebrew word that is translated as simple implies that it means foolish and easily deceived.

As we apply this to recovery we are reminded that we must prudently avoid people, places and programs we know or suspect will cause us anxiety or other trouble. If we don't always have this in our minds, we then run the risk of being deceived and foolishly get involved in something that hurts us.

<u>The Exercise</u> – Take a look back and write a paragraph or two about some of the imprudent choices you made prior to recovery. Then move on to write another paragraph about imprudent choices you have made since you started recovery. In both of these include a one sentence statement indicating if you now believe you had blinders on or were deceived in other ways.

Next write maybe two paragraphs on the subject, "What I am now more prudent about." Speak to the better or wiser choices you are making. Include your thoughts on how this is protecting you and your loved ones from dangers.

Finally write out one paragraph laying out some advice on being prudent for individuals who are dealing with your particular issue.

Sponsor Notes: _____

_____

_____

Useful Feeling Words:

- Careful, Anxious, Afraid, Careless, Troubled

Useful Attitudinal Words:

- Prudence, Cautiousness, Gratitude, Shame, Guilt

My Pre-exercise Notes: _____

_____

_____

_____

The suggested step for Exercise 48 is Step 10.

Exercise 49

Ecclesiastes 5:4-5

Beginning of Integrity

Eccl 5:4-5 - When you vow a vow to God, do not delay paying it, for he has no pleasure in fools. Pay what you vow. It is better that you should not vow than that you should vow and not pay. ESV

Guiding Commentary – These verses come from the middle of a portion of scripture (Ecc 5:1-7) that ends with these words, "Therefore stand in awe of God." Our verses here are part of the reason we ought to be in awe of God.

In Christian recovery we often make promises or bargains with God. We promise that we will "do the work" or we promise that if only God would take care of something we vow to do something in return. Then as we get relief from whatever our situation is, we start to slack off. Ultimately we often end up completely forgetting our promises to God, and basically don't keep our word. The point of considering what God is telling us through this passage is for us to move toward a higher level of personal integrity.

God is saying that we ought not to make hollow, unachievable or rash promises to Him. He doesn't like that, in fact, if we consider that in scripture fools are considered evil in nature, He is basically saying that unkept promises to Him are acts of evil. And that is why He says it is better to not make a vow to Him, than to not fulfill it. It is our contention that personal integrity is a core consideration in our work on our character defects. The start of improving our integrity begins when we make and keep vows to God. It is only after we have begun that work that we will begin to see our integrity improve in our human relationships.

The Exercise – In this exercise we want to confess some personal integrity issues. If we are in Christian recovery, and out of our denial, we know that there are integrity issues in our lives.

Start this exercise by meditating over your life, at least once a day for a whole week, about promises you may have made to God. As you meditate, write some notes in your journal about what God brings to your mind on this subject.

Consider that you may have made direct promises, or prayer promises or bargain based promises; consider them all. Compile for yourself a list of your promises and make a notation as to whether you have kept them.

Now write a short prayer for yourself about your personal integrity with God, and if the following is true include it. "Lord, I want to never break a promise to you again, let today be the beginning of my new awareness about only making promises to you I believe I can fulfill. And Lord, please grant me the power through your Holy Spirit to accomplish this."

Sponsor Notes: _____

_____

_____

Useful Feeling Words:

- Healing, Expectant, Stressed, Confident, Troubled

Useful Attitudinal Words:

- Rebelliousness, Thankfulness, Resentment, Confidence, Anxiety

My Pre-exercise Notes: _____

_____

_____

_____

_____

The suggested step for exercise 49 is step 4.

Exercise 50

Proverbs 12:15

<u>Listen to Avoid Foolishness</u>

Prov 12:15 - The way of a fool is right in his own eyes, but a wise man listens to advice. ESV

<u>Guiding Commentary</u> – Many of us can remember the days when we lived by Frank Sinatra's creed. The crooner sang the theme song of all humanists, "I did it my way." And as far as we know, he did it his way into the pit. We cannot rejoice in that but we can sure understand it. For so long before we wised up, our way was the right way, just like poor old Frank. We thought we were smart as we lied, cheated and stole our way into eventual trouble, and nobody was going to tell us what to do.

Our verse here says it exactly the way it really is, and the only way we discovered actually works in life. It says a fool, "eviyl" in the Hebrew, from which we get the word evil (obviously) does his or her own thing. They don't listen to the counsel of others, but instead make choices to please themselves. Our scripture clearly states that a wise person not only hears, but actively listens to others in life's ongoing difficult choices.

All recovery programs that work contain the "listen to others" ingredient in their recipe for success. Christian recovery stresses that having many godly counselors leads to victory. (See also Proverbs 15:22.)

<u>The Exercise</u> – Write out a paragraph or two about how you used to do things your own way before recovery. In this try to be specific about what choices you made that you knew might be wrong in others' eyes. Try to identify one or two people who tried to talk with you about your activities, choices and selfishness. Answer this question, "Do you believe that you were making mostly evil choices pre-recovery?

In a third and possibly fourth paragraph talk about how hard it was to give up making your own isolating decisions about how life was to be lived. Talk about one or maybe two things you did, after entering recovery, without asking for advice, that didn't go the way you thought. What could you have done differently?

Finally, write out how you handle decisions now. Do you still go it alone, or do you involve others? Do you surround yourself with godly advisors? Name them for the record.

Sponsor Notes: _____

_____

_____

Useful Feeling Words:

- Isolated, Surrounded, Anxious, Embarrassed, Closed

Useful Attitudinal Words:

- Closed-minded, Withdrawn, Resentful, Uncomfortable, Cautiousness

My Pre-exercise Notes: _____

_____

_____

_____

_____

The suggested step for Exercise 50 is Step 4.

Addendum 1

Exercises by Suggested Step

No.	Scripture	Theme	Step	Page
5	Ecc 1:12-14	How are you Striving?	1	12
9	Ecc 8:8	Wickedness Binds	1	20
18	Ecc 3:1	Time for Recovery	1	38
22	Pr 18:1	An Enemy Called Isolation	1	46
23	Ps 88:3-5	Cut Off From God	1	48
8	Ps 119:9	How can I stay pure?	2	18
21	Ps 111:7-10	Believe God?	2	44
28	Ps 51:6	Taking Personal Responsibility	2	58
29	Ps 103:3-5	Hopelessness and Powerlessness	2	60
37	Ps 97:9	Turn to the Supreme One	2	76
3	Pr 1:7	Christian Recovery Begins Here	3	8
4	Pr 2:1-5	Developing Fear of the Lord	3	10
17	Ps 86:11	Teach Me	3	36
30	Ps 121:1-2	Finding Help	3	62
33	Ps 31:7-8	Praying for Deliverance	3	68
1	Ps 103:3-5 (2)	Who Heals, Restores and Renews?	4	4
7	Ecc 2:1	Meaningless Pleasures	4	16
12	Pr 29:6	Evil Snares!	4	26
13	Pr 16:25	I Did it My Way	4	28
31	Pr 3:7-8	Refresh the Body	4	64
39	Ecc 11:4	Recovery Doesn't Just Happen	4	80
49	Ecc 5:4-5	Beginning of Integrity	4	100
50	Pr 12:15	Listen to Avoid Foolishness	4	102
19	Pr 15:22	A Component of Victory	5	40
32	Pr 18:21	The Power of the Tongue	5	66
43	Pr 6:16-19	Abominations to Avoid	5	88
25	Pr 29:1	Stiff Necked Relapse	6	52
11	Ps 138:1-3	Have You Called God?	7	24

Addendum 2

Exercises by Scripture Reference

No.	Scripture	Theme	Step	Page
5	Ecc 1:12-14	How are you Striving?	1	12
7	Ecc 2:1	Meaningless Pleasures	4	16
14	Ecc 2:10-11	Gaining Nothing	10	30
18	Ecc 3:1	Time for Recovery	1	38
44	Ecc 4:9-12	Loners Fall	12	90
49	Ecc 5:4-5	Beginning of Integrity	4	100
26	Ecc 7:3	Seeking Sorrow	7	54
36	Ecc 8:5-6	Time for Amends?	8	74
9	Ecc 8:8	Wickedness Binds	1	20
39	Ecc 11:4	Recovery Doesn't Just Happen	4	80
3	Pr 1:7	Christian Recovery Begins Here	3	8
4	Pr 2:1-5	Developing Fear of the Lord	3	10
42	Pr 3:1-2	Living the Life	10	86
31	Pr 3:7-8	Refresh the Body	4	64
10	Pr 4:23	Guard the Heart	11	22
43	Pr 6:16-19	Abominations to Avoid	5	88
35	Pr 11:20	Becoming a Delight to God	11	72
50	Pr 12:15	Listen to Avoid Foolishness	4	102
16	Pr 14:9	Taking Amends Seriously	8	34
20	Pr 14:21	Helping the Needy	12	42
19	Pr 15:22	A Component of Victory	5	40
13	Pr 16:25	I Did it My Way	4	28
22	Pr 18:1	An Enemy Called Isolation	1	46
32	Pr 18:21	The Power of the Tongue	5	66
40	Pr 20:9	Ongoing Cleansing	10	82
48	Pr 22:3	Prudent Avoidance	10	98
45	Pr 25:8	Be Careful With Amends	9	92
25	Pr 29:1	Stiff Necked Relapse	6	52

Addendum 3

List of Feeling and Attitude Words

Positive Tone/Attitude/Emotion Words

Amiable	Consoling	Friendly	Playful
Amused	Content	Happy	Pleasant
Appreciative	Dreamy	Hopeful	Proud
Authoritative	Ecstatic	Impassioned	Relaxed
Benevolent	Elated	Jovial	Reverent
Brave	Elevated	Joyful	Romantic
Calm	Encouraging	Jubilant	Soothing
Cheerful	Energetic	Lighthearted	Surprised
Cheery	Enthusiastic	Loving	Sweet
Compassionate	Excited	Optimistic	Sympathetic
Complimentary	Exuberant	Passionate	Vibrant
Confident	Fanciful	Peaceful	Whimsical

Negative Tone/Attitude/Emotion Words

Accusing	Choleric	Furious	Quarrelsome
Aggravated	Coarse	Harsh	Shameful
Agitated	Cold	Haughty	Smooth
Angry	Condemnatory	Hateful	Snooty
Apathetic	Condescending	Hurtful	Superficial
Arrogant	Contradictory	Indignant	Surly
Artificial	Critical	Inflammatory	Testy
Audacious	Desperate	Insulting	Threatening
Belligerent	Disappointed	Irritated	Tired
Bitter	Disgruntled	Manipulative	Uninterested
Boring	Disgusted	Obnoxious	Wrathful
Brash	Disinterested	Outraged	
Childish	Facetious	Passive	

Humor-Irony-Sarcasm Tone/Attitude/Emotion Words

Amused	Droll	Mock-heroic	Sardonic
Bantering	Facetious	Mocking	Satiric
Bitter	Flippant	Mock-serious	Scornful
Caustic	Giddy	Patronizing	Sharp
Comical	Humorous	Pompous	Silly
Condescending	Insolent	Quizzical	Taunting
Contemptuous	Ironic	Ribald	Teasing
Critical	Irreverent	Ridiculing	Whimsical
Cynical	Joking	Sad	Wry
Disdainful	Malicious	Sarcastic	

Sorrow-Fear-Worry Tone/Attitude/Emotion Words

Aggravated	Embarrassed	Morose	Resigned
Agitated	Fearful	Mournful	Sad
Anxious	Foreboding	Nervous	Serious
Apologetic	Gloomy	Numb	Sober
Apprehensive	Grave	Ominous	Solemn
Concerned	Hollow	Paranoid	Somber
Confused	Hopeless	Pessimistic	Staid
Dejected	Horrific	Pitiful	Upset
Depressed	Horror	Poignant	
Despairing	Melancholy	Regretful	
Disturbed	Miserable	Remorseful	

Neutral Tone/Attitude/Emotion Words

Admonitory	Dramatic	Intimate	Questioning
Allusive	Earnest	Judgmental	Reflective
Apathetic	Expectant	Learned	Reminiscent
Authoritative	Factual	Loud	Resigned
Baffled	Fervent	Lyrical	Restrained
Callous	Formal	Matter-of-fact	Seductive
Candid	Forthright	Meditative	Sentimental
Ceremonial	Frivolous	Nostalgic	Serious
Clinical	Haughty	Objective	Shocking
Consoling	Histrionic	Obsequious	Sincere
Contemplative	Humble	Patriotic	Unemotional
Conventional	Incredulous	Persuasive	Urgent
Detached	Informative	Pleading	Vexed
Didactic	Inquisitive	Pretentious	Wistful
Disbelieving	Instructive	Provocative	Zealous

This organized list is provided to help those who are working on the exercises in these books. Emotion and attitude words are very useful in helping prepare answers to questions and for mentors, sponsors, coaches and counselors in their work with those in recovery.

Addendum 4

Ten Emotional Needs

During our time in recovery we have noticed time and again a common theme running through the stories we hear. There seems to be some emotional needs that we all have in common and that are so often glaringly not met in those who live a life involving significant compulsive behaviors. This list is provided for sponsors, mentors, counselors or other spiritual guides and the individuals who use this book as an aide in working through issues. As a person works a program or walks through counseling, this list might help unlock some things for them.

These are listed in alphabetical order; different individuals need different amounts of these, and/or have different levels of deficits of these in their life.

- **Acceptance** - deliberate and ready reception with favorable positive response (Rom. 15:7)
- **Affection** - to communicate care and closeness through physical touch (Rom. 16:16)
- **Appreciation** - to communicate with words and feelings a personal gratefulness for another (1 Cor. 11:2)
- **Approval** - to think and speak well of (Rom. 14:18)
- **Attention** - to take thought of another and convey interest and support; to enter into another's world (I Cor. 12:25)
- **Comfort (empathy)** - to come alongside with word, feeling, and touch; to give consolation with tenderness (Rom. 12:15)
- **Encouragement** - to urge forward and positively persuade toward a goal (I Thess. 5:11, Heb. 10:24)
- **Respect** - to value and regard highly; to convey great worth (Phil. 2:4)
- **Security** - confidence of harmony in relationships; free from harm (Rom. 12:16a)
- **Support** - come alongside and gently help carry a load (Gal. 6:2)

Addendum 5

Exercise Record

Use this simple log sheet to keep a record of when you did an exercise and any quick thought you may have about it for your own future reference. It has been helpful to some to go back and do an exercise again a few months after doing it for the first time and comparing their answers.

	Exercise Theme	Date	Short Comment
1	Who Heals, Restores and Renews?		
2	A Perspective on Recovery		
3	Christian Recovery Begins Here		
4	Developing Fear of the Lord		
5	How are you Striving?		
6	Lift up Your Eyes		
7	Meaningless Pleasures		
8	How can I stay pure?		
9	Wickedness Binds		
10	Guard the Heart		
11	Have You Called God?		
12	Evil Snares!		
13	I Did it My Way		
14	Gaining Nothing		
15	Wicked or Righteous?		
16	Taking Amends Seriously		
17	Teach Me		
18	Time for Recovery		
19	A Component of Victory		
20	Helping the Needy		
21	Believe God?		
22	An Enemy Called Isolation		
23	Cut Off From God		

24 Life is Short

25 Stiff Necked Relapse

26 Seeking Sorrow

27 Turning to God

28 Taking Personal Responsibility

29 Hopelessness and Powerlessness

30 Finding Help

31 Refresh the Body

32 The Power of the Tongue

33 Praying for Deliverance

34 Waiting on God

35 Becoming a Delight to God

36 Time for Amends?

37 Turn to the Supreme One

38 Daily Confession

39 Recovery Doesn't Just Happen

40 Ongoing Cleansing

41 Compassion for Defects

42 Living the Life

43 Abominations to Avoid

44 Loners Fall

45 Be Careful With Amends

46 Recovery Has its Own Pace

47 Bless Someone

48 Prudent Avoidance

49 Beginning of Integrity

50 Listen to Avoid Foolishness

Addendum 6 - Example 12 Steps

This is a list of the 12 steps for one of Merimnao's support groups, used by permission of Merimnao Healing Ministry. This particular list is from their Castimonia – Men's Sexual Purity Group, see Castimonia.org for information on them and how to contact the group.

1. **We admitted we were powerless over our addictions and compulsive behaviors, that our lives had become unmanageable.** *"I know that nothing good lives in me, that is, in my sinful nature. For I have the desire to do what is good, but I cannot carry it out."* (Romans 7:18)

2. **We came to believe that a power greater than ourselves could restore us to sanity.** *"For it is God who works in you to will and to act according to his good purpose."* (Philippians 2:13)

3. **We made a decision to turn our lives and our wills over to the care of God.** *"Humble yourselves, therefore, under God's mighty hand, that he may lift you up in due time. Cast all your anxiety on Him because He cares for you."* (1 Peter 5:6-7)

4. **We made a searching and fearless moral inventory of ourselves.** *"Let us examine our ways and test them, and let us return to the LORD."* (Lamentations 3:40)

5. **We admitted to God, to ourselves, and to another human being the exact nature of our wrongs.** *"Therefore confess your sins to each other and pray for each other so that you may be healed."* (James 5:16)

6. **We were entirely ready to have God remove all these defects of character.** *"Humble yourselves before the Lord, and he will lift you up."* (James 4:10)

7. **We humbly ask Him to remove all our shortcomings.** *"If we confess our sins, he is faithful and just and will forgive us our sins and purify us from all unrighteousness."* (1 John 1:9)

8. **We made a list of all persons we had harmed and became willing to make amends to them all.** *"Be kind and compassionate to one another, forgiving each other, just as in Christ, God forgave you."* (Ephesians 4:32)

9. **We made direct amends to such people whenever possible, except when to do so would injure them or others.** *"Be devoted to one another in brotherly love. Honor one another above yourselves. If it is possible, as far as it depends on you, live at peace with everyone."* (Romans 12:10, 18)

10. **We continued to take personal inventory and when we were wrong, promptly admitted it.** *"So, if you think you are standing firm, be careful that you don't fall!"* (1 Corinthians 10:12)

11. **We sought through prayer and meditation to improve our conscious contact with God, praying only for knowledge of His will for us and the power to carry that out.** *"Do not conform any longer to the pattern of this world, but be transformed by the renewing of your mind. Then you will be able to test and approve what God's will is – His good, pleasing, and perfect will."* (Romans 12:2)

12. **Having had a spiritual experience as the result of these steps, we try to carry this message to others and to practice these principles in all our affairs.** *"Praise be to the God and Father of our Lord Jesus Christ, the Father of compassion and the God of all comfort, who comforts us in all our troubles, so that we can comfort those in any trouble with the comfort we ourselves have received from God."* (2 Corinthians 1:3-4)

Addendum 7

The Three Books

There are three books in this series "Recovery Exercises for Christians" each having 50 written exercises for those in the world of Christian recovery to use.

1. Random Scriptures
2. Books of Wisdom
3. Characters of the Bible

Random is a set of exercises that are taken from all over the Bible. Books of Wisdom is 50 exercises taken out of the three books of wisdom, Psalms, Proverbs and Ecclesiastes. Characters is a set of 50 exercises based on the lives of real people as described in scripture.

The development of the three books occurred as we worked with sponsees on the early part of their programs, and noticed that there was a need for some scripture centered study material. This came from some core beliefs we have. First, that scripture is the infallible source for all written wisdom, given to us by God Himself for use as a guide to real life. Second, that the Bible itself is the book of recovery; it contains the story of God's work to recover the entire human race. This makes our God the God of recovery.

It is our contention that all peoples in all nations ought to consider themselves in recovery, because we believe this is true:

Rom 3:23 - For all have sinned and fall short of the glory of God. ESV

Every human has fallen short, and so all need to be recovered. We hope that these three books contribute to that happening in some people's lives.

My Notes

Use the next few pages to write out your random thoughts, individual musings, deep meditations or personal revelations. Be sure to date them for your records.

My Notes - Page 2

My Notes - Page 3

My Notes - Page 4